D0043358

the tropical fish
handbook

the
tropical fish
handbook

David Goodwin

magnet™
& steel

© 2014 Magnet & Steel Ltd

This edition published by Magnet & Steel Ltd

Printed 2014

This book is distributed in the UK by
Magnet & Steel Ltd
Unit 6
Vale Business Park
Cowbridge
CF71 7PF

sales@magnetsteel.com

ISBN: 978-1-907337-73-4

All rights reserved. This book is protected by copyright. No part of it
may be reproduced, stored in a retrieval system, or transmitted in any
form or by any means, without the prior permission in writing of the
Publisher, nor be circulated in any form of binding or cover other
than that in which it is published and without a similar condition
including this condition being imposed on the subsequent Publisher

Printed by Printworks Global Ltd., London/Hong Kong

contents

Introduction

Watching fish swimming around an aquarium is extremely calming and peaceful, especially after a stressful day. Having spent time and money designing and setting up an aquarium, it is very satisfying to watch the fruits of your labours flourish and possibly breed. Fish undoubtedly have a soothing and therapeutic effect upon the human psyche.

Introduction

I have been keeping fish for more than 30 years. I started by buying some second-hand equipment and soon progressed to having a fish house in my garden with 48 tanks, ranging from 24 x 12 x 12 in (60 x 30 x 30cm) to 48 x 15 x 12 in (122 x 38 x 30cm). In my house I had two 96 x 24 x 24 in (244 x 60 x 60cm) aquariums and a 48 x 20 x 16 in (122 x 50 x 40cm) marine system. I used my third bedroom as a fish breeding room in which there were another 18 tanks of various sizes. I then bred many different types of fish and sold them into the trade.

I became a member of a local club, eventually working on the committee and progressed to become a fish judge. I gave talks and slide shows on various subjects within an 80-mile (130-kilometre) radius of my home. I then worked on the committee of an area group and organised conventions in southeast England for ten years. At some point in the middle of all this I set up my first shop, which allowed me to access many rare and beautiful fish, and I began to specialise in the more unusual species. I have also been fortunate enough to collect and study fish from the wild on a trip I made with some friends to Africa.

In 1996, I bought a wholesaling business and now have a fish house with over 700 tanks, holding at any given time approximately 600 species of fish. I import from all over the world, ranging from the Far East to South America and a few places in between. All this experience has

given me a great deal of knowledge, but I am aware that there is always someone out there who knows more. One of the many things that I really enjoy about this hobby is that you can never know it all and every day I learn something new.

Fish-keeping is an ideal hobby for adults and children alike. It is also a practical and enjoyable way for children to learn the responsibility of caring for a living creature and it will help you to bond with your children. With so many aquariums being placed in the waiting rooms of doctor's surgeries, dental surgeries, waiting rooms and hospital wards, it shows that there is a therapeutic side to keeping fish. Personal stress levels are reduced and we feel better within ourselves – as anyone involved in Feng Shui will confirm. The satisfaction of seeing your fish grow and breed, and then hopefully grow into the next generation is very rewarding.

Fish do not require a great deal of maintenance, not like grooming a dog and having to take it for walks each day, for example. The amount of time and money that you spend on the initial purchase and design of your aquarium is far outweighed by the pleasure derived from working with such a peaceful environment.

General Advice

First, find a well-stocked specialist shop with knowledgeable and helpful staff. It is worth shopping around to compare prices and stocks. When purchasing your first aquarium and other equipment buy the very best that you can afford. This will always save you money in the long run. Carefully plan the size of the aquarium that you want and work out how much it will all cost. (Every fish-keeper that I know has wanted a larger aquarium within six months.) When the shopkeeper suggests a specific size of pump or heater thermostat, buy the next size up. By doing this, your equipment will work more easily and last longer.

General running costs are quite low. Some day-to-day foods can be prepared from your own fridge or freezer (see page 15), and some live foods such as daphnia or Cyclops can be collected from local ponds or streams. For decoration, a few large nicely shaped pebbles can be collected during a walk on the beach, but you must always remember to boil, scrub and thoroughly sterilise them before placing them in the aquarium. Pieces of rock or slate purchased from your local dealer can be bonded together using aquarium silicone sealant to make caves or hiding places. Short pieces of plastic pipe, such as sink waste pipe, can be bonded together using silicone sealant. Coat the pipes with a thin layer of the same sealant and then coat them in gravel so that they blend into the aquarium set-up, again to make hideaways for your fish. Leave the finished pipe-work to one side for 24 hours for it to cure and it will then be ready to place in your aquarium.

By going to one shop regularly, you will build up a relationship with the staff and generally receive better service. Check that the shop maintains its fish tanks properly and never buy fish that appear to be ailing or unhealthy. If a shop has some tanks marked 'In Quarantine', do not be put off by this as it shows that the staff are keeping a good check on the quality of their fish. You can always ask for the fish to be put to one side and buy them when they are ready. Make sure that the fish you intend to purchase have no obvious sores on them. Do not be afraid to ask questions about the fish, plants or equipment that you are thinking of buying. Your children will probably be keen to help install the new aquarium but you should always supervise them closely, particularly if chemicals or electrical equipment are involved.

(Tip: Do not use bathroom sealant in your aquarium. It contains a variety of colour pigments that are toxic to fish.)

Water quality

'Tap water is meant for drinking, not for keeping fish in'. This is an adage that I have heard only too often. Fortunately, in most cases, we can do something about this quite easily, as you will see. Water quality is something that we all take for granted but it varies greatly across the country. The acid or alkali levels, and thus the pH value, depend on the source of the water. On a pH scale, 0 is the acid end of the range and 10 the alkali end. A reading of between 6.8 and 7.0 is regarded as neutral.

Aquarium fish must have water with the correct pH. If it is incorrect the fish will be exceptionally unhappy in the environment, and in some instances will die if it is much too low or much too high. For example, most of the River Amazon is on the acidic side of neutral, whereas the lakes in the Rift Valley in Africa have very hard water, with pH readings never lower than 8. This is why you must always check the water requirements of the individual fish that you wish to keep and not put them through any unnecessary pain or stress.

As a guideline for a general community aquarium, a pH level of somewhere between 6.6 and 7.5 should be adequate. In some areas, the water is referred to as 'soft', meaning that it is slightly acidic because it lacks calcium and various other minerals. If soap lathers easily in your tap water, you probably live in an area of soft water. 'Hard' water is drawn through substrate in mainly limestone, sandstone or chalk areas, which gives it an alkaline pH value. Tap water may appear chalky or cloudy because of the calcium content. Soap does not lather so readily. There are two types of hardness: temporary hardness and permanent hardness. Temporary hardness is caused by the presence of calcium and magnesium bicarbonates, which can be removed. Permanent hardness derives from a number of sulphates, such as calcium and magnesium, in the water, as well as the chlorides that are used for purification of the water supply.

Testing and altering pH value

There are a number of reasonably priced test kits, whether they are dip strips, liquid chemicals or tablets. Electronic meters are also available to measure pH values. A local supplier will always recommend items and will also be able to give you a good idea of what pH values to expect in your area. Boiling the water and allowing it to cool before putting it into your aquarium will easily remove temporary hardness. Under no circumstances should you place boiling or hot water into your aquarium. Permanent hardness can be removed but this is not advisable for tropical fish. If you need to raise the pH, add sodium bicarbonate in small amounts and constantly check until the reading is correct. Acidic buffers can also be purchased.

Toxins

Toxins can build up in an aquarium from decaying waste, overcrowding and inefficient filtration and overfeeding. Nitrites and ammonia are highly toxic to fish, even at very low levels. Nitrites are created by lack of oxygen and are a highly poisonous toxin, even if they are present in a weak concentration. A combination of high levels of ammonium and a pH reading of over 6.8 helps create ammonia in the aquarium. Low ammonium levels on their own are not too much of a problem but they will increase if there is decaying waste matter, combined with too many fish in the aquarium and overfeeding.

Very low levels of ammonia are highly toxic to your fish. These toxins can be avoided very easily by keeping the number of fish consistent with the size of the aquarium, and ensuring that the filtration system is efficient. Feed the fish little and often. Partial water changes are essential, and should be done by replacing 25 per cent per month or preferably 10

per cent per week. Test kits are readily available and you should do tests on a regular basis, weekly being best. If the reading is too high, replace 25 per cent of the water immediately and test 30 minutes later. If the reading is still higher than normal, change a further 25 per cent of the water. Check the aquarium for dead and decaying fish and get rid of them straight away.

Fish can build up a resistance to high levels of nitrite and ammonia. This will generally happen if the fish stocking levels are reasonably low but no water changes are done at all. Over a period of time the toxic levels increase very slowly and the fish become adjusted to them. When that happens if you then buy new fish and place them in the aquarium, within a very short time, sometimes within only a matter of an hour or two, the new fish die because they cannot withstand the high levels of these toxins. The first person you blame is the shopkeeper from whom you purchased the fish. The only way to detect these toxins is to test the water regularly.

The best way to prevent the build up of toxins is to do regular water changes. Your aquariums can be filled with water from a number of different sources. Tap water is the usual source but as it is chemically treated to make it suitable for human consumption it should be de-chlorinated, using a de-chlorinater from your local supplier, before it is used in an aquarium. Alternatively, it can be aerated in a holding container for 24 hours, which also ensures that the water adjusts to the same temperature as the aquarium. Distilled water is another source but this is a very expensive way of filling an aquarium and the water lacks many of the base minerals required by fish, although distilled water can be used as a small percentage of the water volume in breeding tanks for some species.

Rainwater is a useful source if you live in a rural area but urban rain will inevitably contain too many toxins. Collect rainwater in a wooden or plastic butt. Always allow it to settle for two to three hours and never drain from the bottom but from about 6 in (15cm) from the base. Reverse osmosis (RO water) is filtered through a semi-permeable membrane that filters out up to 90 per cent of the base minerals and impurities in a tap water supply. The filtration process will reduce the level of the pH and must therefore be tested and treated accordingly. You will need to raise the pH if you use RO water, so add small amounts of sodium bicarbonate and constantly check the readings until they are at the level that is correct for your fish.

A wide variety of foods is available.

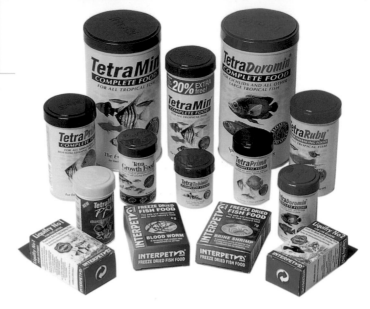

Foods and Feeding

There are many different types of food available. Many fish need specific vitamins and other nutrients on a daily basis that can be provided by a varied diet. Buy only the best quality flake foods available. There is an extensive range with some feeds including additives such as spirulina, for algae-eating fish, colour enhancers to bring out the best colours in your fish and low level medications to maintain their general health.

Flake foods are also available in different sizes for larger fish. Begin with a standard staple food and then learn about the individual requirements of your fish. Always keep three or four different types of food available. Do not just feed flake food to your fish; like us they prefer a varied diet. Dried food is also available as pellets, tablets or freeze-dried.

Pellet food is mainly for surface feeders and bottom feeders. There are different sizes to choose from depending on the size of your fish. Some of the pellets contain air to make them float and are ideal for fish that have an upturned mouth to feed from the surface. Other pellets sink quite quickly to the bottom and, as they become saturated, will soften up for the fish to feed on. Tablet food will also normally sink to the bottom, making it ideal for fish like corydoras and many other catfish. In most cases, you can also soak the tablet for a very short time and then press it to the inside of the glass and your free-swimming fish will get used to coming and feeding from it. Freeze-dried foods are very useful if you are unable to obtain a supply of live foods such as bloodworms, tubifex and black mosquito larvae.

Live foods

Unfortunately, some aquatic shops do not have enough sales to warrant stocking live foods so it may be difficult to find a supplier. There are many live foods available, such as tubifex, daphnia, bloodworms, glassworms, brine shrimp, black mosquito larvae and river shrimp. Only ever buy as much as your fish will want for one day unless you are prepared to maintain these foods. You will have to refrigerate some of them. Adding this type of food to the aquarium will provoke a feeding frenzy among the fish who will hunt for it after it has all been devoured. Always rinse this type of food with fresh water before placing it in the aquarium. Beware of glassworms. Although very small, they can be predatory if placed in an aquarium with very small fish fry.

Frozen food

Frozen foods are probably the most convenient way to feed your fish. The many varieties of frozen food now available will feed just about any species. Multi-menu packs contain four or five different types of food in a handy blister pack, which means that one small cube can be used at a time.

Kitchen food

Fish can also eat certain vegetables and meat in small portions. Vegetable- and algae-eating fish love cooked garden peas. These can be fed to your fish when you have cooked them for your own meal and allowed a few of them to cool right off. Squeeze the pea shell so that all the soft insides come out and feed them in small amounts. The larger outer leaves of a soft lettuce can also be used. Rinse them under cold water, and then dip them into boiling water for a couple of seconds. By attaching a small weight to the bottom of the leaf, it will sink to the bottom of your aquarium for your fish to relish. Carnivorous fish enjoy beef heart. Freeze a small quantity and when it is solid, grate off just enough for one feed. Defrost it and then feed to the fish.

Other foods

Earthworms are an excellent food for larger fish. They must be cleaned before feeding by placing them in a very shallow saucer of milk for a couple of minutes and then draining them on a paper towel for a further five minutes. They can be chopped up or diced before being added to the aquarium. Mealworms are another very good food but only for larger fish. Use a few at a time, as they are a very fatty food and will foul the

Proprietary treatments are available to combat the most common fish ailments.

aquarium water very quickly if they are not eaten. Live crickets are a very tasty meal for really good-sized fish.

Feed your fish at the same time each day; the fish will get to know the person who is feeding them. It might be sensible to restrict feeding to just one person, which will ensure that the fish are not overfed. If there is still any food left in the tank after 10 minutes, you are overfeeding. Scoop out the food to avoid fouling the tank.

Diseases

To reduce the risk of any type of disease in the main tank, you should purchase a small quarantine tank. Any new fish should be placed in it for about 10 days or until you are sure that the fish is healthy. It can then be moved to the main tank. If a fish from the main tank requires treatment, you can use the quarantine tank to treat the problem. A quarantine tank only needs to be very basic; being filtered and aerated, possibly with an internal power filter to do both jobs and then heated to the correct temperature. Other than this, the tank can be bare. There are basically three different types of disease: bacterial, parasitic and viral. Fungal problems are usually a secondary disease.

White spot – Ichthyopthirius

This is by far the most common problem in an aquarium and is normally caused by shock or stress. Simply catching or transporting the fish, banging on the front of the aquarium or large changes in temperature between one aquarium and another can cause this. The symptoms are that the fish will start flicking itself upon any item in the aquarium; tiny pinhead-sized white spots will then appear on the body and fins. If left untreated, the fish can die.

There are many proprietary treatments available to cure white spot. Alternatively, increase the temperature of the heater by 10 degrees for a period of 24 hours and then turn the control back down to the normal setting which will normally cure this problem. Do not put hot water or cold water in the aquarium to increase or decrease the temperature. Let the heater thermostat heat it up and then allow it to cool to its normal temperature naturally.

Velvet – Oodinium

This is similar to white spot but is normally restricted to the sides and crown of the back. The spots are very fine, like dust and are gold in colour. It is easier to see while the infected fish is swimming and turning in the light. It is very easy to cure with a proprietary medication. If you have a quarantine tank, place the fish in it and treat with 1 oz (28gm) of aquarium salt per gallon (4.5 litres) of water, which should cure it within two or three days. If it proves stubborn, add an additional 1 oz (28gm) of aquarium salt per gallon (4.5 litres) to the aquarium. After another day or two, you should find that the fish is cured.

Ulceration

This disease causes small lumps to appear underneath the skin and slowly grow like a boil. The skin will break open leaving unsightly wounds. The best cure is to place the fish in a quarantine tank in clean water, raise the temperature slightly and then ask an aquatic shopkeeper for some recommended medication. It will take time and patience to cure this problem.

Tip: If you keep mollies, especially black mollies, be aware that they require some salt in the water. If this is not present, they will show small white patches on their body from time to time, similar to white spot. Treating for white spot will not cure this. Another way round this, so that you do not have to put salt in your aquarium, is to place the affected mollies in a salt bath for a short time. Use a small container and put 4 teaspoons of aquarium salt in a gallon of water, stir it thoroughly and allow it to dissolve. Place the fish in it for 20 minutes and then replace them in their aquarium. If you do this once a day for three or four days, the white patches should vanish. Make up a new solution every day.

Gill infections

This type of infection can be created by either bacterial or parasitic problems. Study the problem, note the symptoms and consult a local dealer who will recommend some medication. A bacterial remedy will not cure a parasitic problem and vice versa.

Fungal problems

Spores of fungi are always present in aquariums and healthy fish are usually unaffected by them. Unhealthy fish are more susceptible, however. Mouth fungus can be a problem in bottom feeders in an aquarium with a crushed gravel substrate. Body fungus can appear if the fish are roughly handled. Their outer skin can be removed by abrasive handling in the net or by fighting other fish. If the skin's protective layer is damaged or removed, fungus spores will go straight to work. Careful handling can prevent this, as can the use of round gravel as a substrate. Problems occur in the best-kept tanks. If your fish become ill, do not panic but try to solve the problem as quickly as possible.

Tip: Wear plastic or medical gloves when treating the fish so that you do not damage your skin if you spill chemicals or treatments. Check the lifespan of any treatment. The lifespan of some chemicals can be very short once you have opened them. When they are out of date, dispose of them carefully and correctly and buy replacements straight away.

The Aquarium

There are now a number of different types of aquarium available. There is the standard all-glass variety, which is quite basic; the deluxe aquarium, which generally has its own built-in hood with sliding glass shelving inside (and normally you can buy a matching cabinet); and the latest design, which is a one-piece tank built from acrylics. All these are all very good – it's just a matter of choice and partly depends on the size of the area where the aquarium is to be positioned. The larger the aquarium that you can buy the better, as it is easier to maintain a larger volume of water – disease in an aquarium with a small volume of water quickly becomes a major problem.

Where you place your aquarium is quite important. Placing it in direct sunlight, behind a door, in a very dark corner or in front of a radiator is not a good idea. Lots of algal growth will occur if the aquarium is positioned in a sunny area and you will always be cleaning the inside. Placing it with a door that opens onto it will cause problems. If the door is opened too quickly, you are liable to damage the aquarium and if it is constantly knocking the aquarium you will create shock and stress to the fish and also cause disease. If the aquarium is placed in a dark corner, you will not be able to appreciate the fish and finally, with a radiator behind the aquarium you will build up unnecessary heat, which will again cause problems.

Setting up the Aquarium

How you set up and fill your aquarium is really only limited by your own imagination. Try not to use spa or sharp gravel as this can cause damage to the mouths of the fish when they feed from the bottom. I recommend pea gravel because it is smooth and round. It comes in a variety of sizes and I generally find that the ½-³⁄₂ in (3-4mm) or about ¼ in (6-7mm) are the best to use. These are also very good from the filtration point of view, as they allow a much smoother flow of water through the filter bed. The gravel should be thoroughly washed and cleaned of all the dust that comes with it. Any rocks or stones that you are going to use inside the aquarium also need to be checked to see that they are okay to use. An easy check once you have thoroughly cleaned them is to pour a few drops of vinegar onto the rock and see if it fizzes or bubbles. If it does, then do not use it. If it just rolls off without any reaction, then wash it again thoroughly and put it to one side ready to use.

Figure 1

If you are going to place a backing picture sheet on the aquarium, now is the time to do it because when the aquarium is full, you will not be able to move it. Make sure that the stand or cabinet that you are going to place the aquarium on is in the correct position and is also safe and stable. Lay a sheet of polystyrene on it and cut it to the correct size so that there is no overhang. Place the aquarium on the cabinet and ensure that it is completely square. For safety, get someone to help you lift the aquarium into place.

Filter plates

Generally, I use under gravel filter plates and you now need to place the blanking plug into one end (figure 1) and screw the uplift tube base into the filter plate (figure 2).

Figure 2

Figure 3

Figure 4

Figure 5

The uplift tube should then be fitted tightly into the uplift base (figure 3) and the whole plate can then carefully be placed into the aquarium, covering the whole of the base (figures 4 & 5).

Ensure that the base of the aquarium is totally clean or the filter plate will not seal to the base of the aquarium and will not work efficiently. The plate can be bonded to the base of the aquarium if you wish, using aquarium sealant but you will have to wait for 24 hours for it to set properly before any more can be done.

The washed gravel can now be placed on top of the filter plate (figures 6 & 7), ensuring that no gravel particles get below it. The gravel needs to be to a depth of 2½ –3 in (7–8cm) for it to work efficiently as a filter base.

The air line can now be threaded through the uplift tube crown (figure 8) and the air stone attached to the end of it (figure 9).

The air stone is then slid into the uplift tube (figure 10), the crown is pushed onto the top of the uplift tube and the air line is then pushed all of the way down, until it just touches the bottom of the aquarium (figure 11).

The other end of the air line is then connected to the air pump (figure 12).

Alternatively, you can use an internal power filter (figure 13). This will come with a full set of instructions on how to put it together and install it. Generally, they are placed into one corner of the aquarium and attached to the glass using the suction pads supplied about two-thirds of the way up the tank.

The heater thermostat is the next item to be installed. The suction caps for this have to be put together (figure 14) and then placed on the heater thermostat (figure 15).

Figure 6

Figure 7

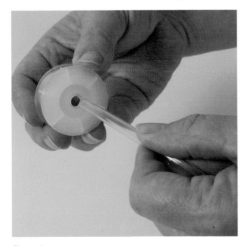

Figure 8

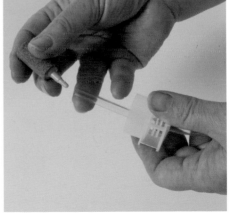

Figure 9

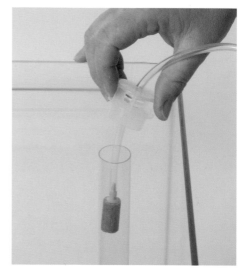

Figure 10

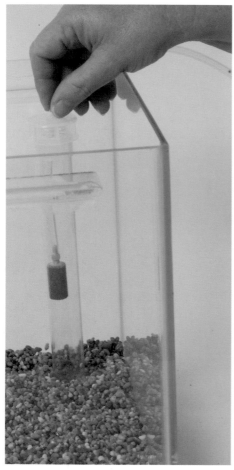

Figure 11

Figure 12

This is then placed on the back glass of the aquarium at an angle of 45 degrees (figure 16). The reason for this is that if the heater thermostat is upright the heat will rise over the thermostat and it will give a false reading to itself, and so will not work efficiently. You must also ensure that at no time is the heater part of this unit covered by the gravel, as this will cause it to burn itself out.

At this time, any bogwood or other solid décor can be put into the aquarium so that you can get the correct placing for it (figure 17).

Figure 13

Figure 14

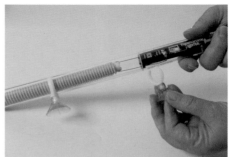

Figure 15

Figure 16

Figure 17

Filling the tank

Having positioned your decorations, now you should start filling the
aquarium with water. Obviously you do not want to dislodge any of the
décor or move the gravel about if you have shaped it. To avoid this, place
a small saucer or dish (figure 18) into the aquarium and then pour water
into this until the aquarium is about half full (figure 19).

Take the plate or dish that you have used and start placing into
position the plants that you have bought for your aquarium. Make sure
that only the root of the plant is below the top level of the gravel. While

Figure 18

Figure 19

Figure 20

Figure 21

Figure 22

Figure 23

Figure 24

Figure 25

Figure 26

Figure 27

Figure 28

the water level is low, you can move the plants about until you are happy with your design without water spilling all over the top and making a mess (Figures 20-26).

Once you have completed this, the dish can be placed back into the aquarium and you can continue to fill it with water until the level is at the stress bars (figures 27-30).

Figure 29

Figure 30

Lighting

It is now time to put your lighting in place and make all of the connections to the power supply. There are various cable tidies on the market with switch units that will enable you to turn the lighting and the air pump on and off. Do not at any stage of the installation process have any electrical items inside the aquarium connected to a power supply until you are happy with the design. When you have finished and everything is correct, double check. Make sure of all the connections, place the condensation cover on top of the aquarium, put the hood into place and wipe up any excess water that may be on the glass.

When you turn on the power supply you should see that the lighting comes on, the air pump is working and blowing lots of air into the aquarium and a light on the heater thermostat is showing. You will now have to leave your aquarium to run for at least 24–36 hours, so that it can become fully aerated and up to temperature. The temperature should be set to run at 75°F (24°C). It will assist the plants to settle in and straighten up if you leave the light on for this time.

When the aquarium has settled put some aquarium conditioner into it and leave for a further 24 hours so that it can be fully mixed into the water. The water should be crystal clear by this time but if there is any cloudiness, turn off all the power to the aquarium and replace 25 per cent of the water. Turn the power back on and leave it for a further 24 hours to settle.

Figure 31

Buying your first fish

When this is done, you are now ready to go to your supplier and buy your first batch of fish. Because of the raw water quality, you must ensure that the first fish that you purchase are very hardy. Do not buy fish such as neon tetras or cardinal tetras as they tend not to last very long. Your supplier should be able to help you choose by offering you a good selection of tough, hardy fish.

When you get the fish home, float the bag (figure 31) in the aquarium for 20 minutes to equalise the temperature. Then undo the bag and put a small amount of water into it from the aquarium and leave for a further 15 minutes and then repeat the process again Finally, gently tip the contents of the bag into the aquarium. Let the fish settle for 24 hours before you feed them for the first time.

Aquatic Plants

There many truly beautiful aquatic plants but unfortunately we only get to see very few of them. Most of the plants shown on the next few pages are easy to keep once your aquarium is established with a good bacterial substrate. Some of the plants are known as bog or marsh plants and do not always easily transfer to a totally immersed environment but it can be done. They can, of course, just be used for a short time as a decorative plant and then thrown away.

Aponogeton crispus

Plants are valuable to the fish as they are used as places where they can hide, or rest and sometimes breed in. Natural light is obviously the best source of light but if you have too much your plants will be covered in algae, which can be very unsightly. A combination of different lighting tubes should be used for the best plant growth and here again your local supplier can recommend the best varieties. If you have multiple tubes on your aquarium, try to set them up with individual timers so that they come on and go off at different times creating a dawn and dusk environment. Change

New Giant Twisted Vallis

the lighting tubes on a regular basis, every 6–9 months. You will always get the best from them and they are also not very expensive. Different tubes give off light at different parts of the colour spectrum, which as humans we cannot see, but the plants certainly benefit from this. Generally, the colour of the plant will indicate how much light it needs. The darker the leaf the less light it requires and vice versa.

Congo Leaf Plant

Nana Plant

Madagascar Lace Leaf Plant

Pigmy Chain Sword

Wheat Plant

Green Dracena

Umbrella Fern Plant

Bronze Bacopa

Hygrophila

Baby Tears Bacopa

Arrowhead

Fountain Plant

Purple Stricta

Moneywort

Hairgrass

Green & White Dracena

Green Cabomba

Yellow Striped
Acorus

Elodea

Giant Corkscrew Vallis

Red Dracena

Indian Fern

Red Radican

Amazon Sword

Water Wisteria

Bog Moss

Red Ambullia

Red Ludwigia

Alternanthera

Straight Vallis

Bogwood with Java Moss

Bogwood with Bacopa

Caring for your plants

They need to be fed in the same way as you would feed your houseplants. There are number of different types of food available in different forms, such as liquid, tablets and pellets. Do not use houseplant feeds because they may poison the fish. You can also install a CO2 system into your aquarium, which is excellent for your plants although it can prove expensive. This is the latest and most efficient way of care for your plants.

General Information

This book is intended to be a general introduction to everyday fish-keeping. I have tried to minimise the use of technical terms and information, although this is not possible in every area. I have listed both the Latin and common name for the fish where possible. Some fish have many common or local names and it is impossible to list them all. Some fish will be imported without any common name and the importer will create a common name with which his buyers can associate. The Latin name consists of a genus (or family) name and a species name which is the individual name of that fish within that family. For example, the Pink Kissing Gourami has a Latin name *Helastoma temminkii*. *Helastoma* is the genus name and *temminkii* is the species name.

Fish Anatomy

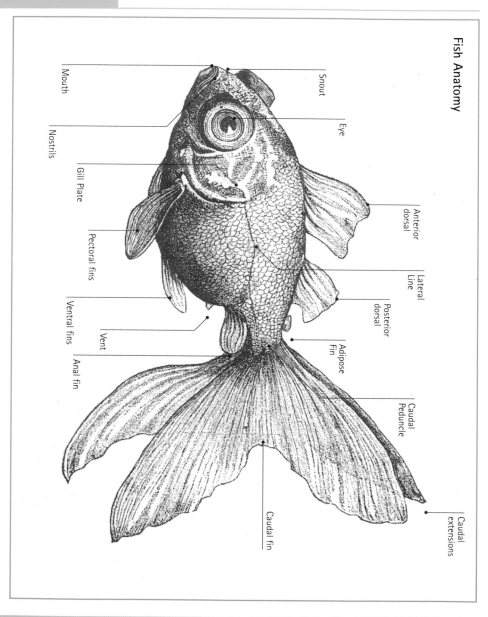

Snout

Eye

Mouth

Nostrils

Gill Plate

Pectoral fins

Ventral fins

Vent

Anal fin

Anterior dorsal

Lateral Line

Posterior dorsal

Adipose Fin

Caudal Peduncle

Caudal extensions

Caudal fin

CALCULATIONS AND IMPERIAL TO METRIC CONVERSIONS

To calculate the surface area of the aquarium:
Multiply the length x width = surface area
(In an unfiltered aquarium, you should allow 12 in (77cm) square of surface area to
1in (2.5cm) in length of fish as a stocking level.

To calculate the cubic volume of the aquarium:
Multiply the length x width x height = cubic volume.
To calculate the water volume of the aquarium:
Imperial measurement – multiply the length x width x height x 6.23
(Do not forget to deduct the depth of the substrate from your measurements.)

To calculate the weight of the aquarium, including the water:
Imperial measurement – multiply the length x width x height x 6.23 x 10

To convert Centigrade into Fahrenheit:
Multiply by $^9/_5$ and add 32

To convert Fahrenheit into Centigrade:
Subtract 32 and multiply x $^5/_9$

1 imperial gallon of water weighs 10lb (4.5kg)

1 imperial gallon of water = 4.54 litres

1 litre of water weighs 1kg (2.2lb)
the species: the red–tailed black shark, for example, is *Labeo bicolo*,
Labeo being the genus and *bicolo* the species.

the
fish
directory

Albino Glowlight Tetra / *Hemigrammus erythrozonus*
Albino

ORIGIN
south america

TEMPERATURE RANGE
73–79°F (23–26°C)

COMMUNITY
excellent

ADULT SIZE
female 1 ³/₄ in (4.5cm)
male 1 ¹/₂ in (4cm)

DIET
all foods

EASE OF KEEPING
9/10

PH RANGE
6.8–7.5

This albino tetra is a very peaceful and beautiful fish that prefers to be in small shoals of about 10–15. The male is quite slim. However, when it is well fed and maintained, the female develops a very plump belly. When first introduced into your aquarium these fish will be quite nervous of their new surrounding and will take a day or two to settle down. They like to have plenty of fine-leafed plants in the aquarium to hide amongst when they feel threatened. The fish are generally only bred commercially as they are quite difficult to spawn. If you are fortunate enough to breed them, they scatter their eggs all over the substrate. However, they will then go looking for them after they have finished laying and eat the eggs.

Feeding
They will take all types of food, but thrive on a wide variety of flakes, frozen and live foods. Make sure that their food is broken down small enough for them to eat.

Albino Lemon Tetra / *Hyphessobrycon pulchiprinnis Albino*

Again, this tetra is much happier to be within small shoals of its own kind in your community aquarium - somewhere between 5-10 fish is a good number. When food is at hand, they are usually one of the first to find it. In the wild, albino fish are generally regarded as weak and other fish frequently target them. This is also partly due to the lack of food in the wild. In your aquarium, however, this does not occur because food is abundant and the fish are fed on a regular basis. With their bright red eye and translucent body, they are a very attractive fish to keep.

Feeding

They will take all types of food, but thrive on a wide variety of flakes, frozen and live foods. Make sure that their food is broken down small enough for them to eat.

ORIGIN
south america

TEMPERATURE RANGE
73–79°F (23–26°C)

COMMUNITY
very good

ADULT SIZE
female 1 ³/₄ in (4.5cm)
male 1 ³/₄ in (4.5cm)

DIET
all foods

EASE OF KEEPING
9/10

PH RANGE
6.8–7.5

TETRA

Albino X Ray Tetra / *Pristella riddlei Albino*

ORIGIN
south america

TEMPERATURE RANGE
73–79°F (23–26°C)

COMMUNITY
excellent

ADULT SIZE
female 1 ³/₄ in (4.5cm)
male 1 ³/₄ in (4.5cm)

DIET
all foods

EASE OF KEEPING
9/10

PH RANGE
6.8–7.5

Albinoism in any living creature is generally seen as a genetic failure but in this case it is just a total lack of colour pigmentation. As you can see from the first three fish in this directory, they are beautiful in their own right. In the wild, albinos are quite rare but they do occur naturally. As a result of commercial breeding, we are able to get quite a high percentage of albino fish from any given spawning so hobbyists can have the pleasure of keeping these fine fish.

When attempting to breed these fish you will find that if you pair up and spawn two albinos you will not get 100 per cent albino fry, but something in the order of 25 per cent albino and 75 per cent standard fish because of their genetic make up. However, out of the 75 per cent you are more liable to have fish with other faults within them. But they are no harder to keep than the standard variety of their species and it does appear that because of their albinoism they are naturally quicker to hide from possible predators.

Feeding

They will take all types of food, but thrive on a wide variety of flakes, frozen and live foods. Make sure that their food is broken down small enough for them to eat.

Black Eyed X Ray Tetra / *Pristella riddlei Black Eye*

As with the other X-ray tetras shown, this is another hardy community tetra that you can easily add to your aquarium. The eye is totally black and stands out against the translucent body. There are splashes of yellow and black in the dorsal and anal fin and shades of red in the tail. Again, for them to look their best, a small shoal is the best way to keep them in your aquarium. They are a very quiet, peaceful and unassuming fish that like to have plenty of fine-leafed plants such as cabomba or bogmoss to swim amongst.

Feeding

They will take all types of food, but thrive on a wide variety of flakes, frozen and live foods. Make sure that their food is broken down small enough for them to eat.

ORIGIN
south america

TEMPERATURE RANGE
73–79°F (23–26°C)

COMMUNITY
excellent

ADULT SIZE
female 1 ³/₄ in(4.5cm
male 1 ³/₄ in (4.5cm

DIET
all foods

EASE OF KEEPING
9/10

PH RANGE
6.8–7.5

Black Line Tetra / *Paracheirodon scholzei*

ORIGIN
south america

TEMPERATURE RANGE
73–79°F (23–26°C)

COMMUNITY
Good

ADULT SIZE
female 2 ½ in (6.5cm)
male 1 ¾ in (4.5cm)

DIET
all foods

EASE OF KEEPING
10/10

PH RANGE
6.8–7.5

Unfortunately, when we photographed this fish it did not like the tank we had it in and so would not colour up properly. Normally it would have an exceptionally black line running from its tail through to the back of its head and bright silvery scaling that makes it stand out in the aquarium. Both males and females are very solid and thick-bodied, although it is very easy to distinguish the difference between the two. The females are always plumper. Four or five of these fish as a small shoal are quite adequate. They are apt to chase in the aquarium but in a group will chase amongst themselves and just keep the other fish in the aquarium on the move. They are not truly aggressive but will fin nip if on their own.

Feeding

They will take all types of food, but thrive on a wide variety of flakes, frozen and live foods. They will be one of the first to feed when food is placed in the tank. Be careful not to overfeed.

Blue Tetra / *Hyphessobrycon boehlkea*

These fish will always take up to a week to really settle into any aquarium. They do not like to be moved but once they have been in the aquarium for a short time will be fine. This species is called the Blue tetra but the body has colours running from lilac through to blue and it is a very beautiful fish to look at. They also have bright white tips to the tail and dorsal fin. White spot can be a minor problem with this fish but with its colouration will be easily seen and then can be dealt with accordingly. If the water quality in your aquarium becomes a problem for whatever reason, this will be one of the first to suffer from it, but this can signal that all is not well and give you the opportunity to rectify it quickly.

Feeding

They will take all types of food, but thrive on a wide variety of flakes, frozen and live foods. Make sure that their food is broken down small enough for them to eat.

ORIGIN
south america

TEMPERATURE RANGE
73–79°F (23–26°C)

COMMUNITY
good

ADULT SIZE
female 2 ¹/₂ in (6.5cm)
male 2 ¹/₂ in (6.5cm)

DIET
all foods

EASE OF KEEPING
8/10

PH RANGE
6.8–7.5

TETRA

Buenos Aries Tetra / *Hemigrammus caudovittatus*

ORIGIN
south america

TEMPERATURE RANGE
73–79°F (23–26°C)

COMMUNITY
good with larger fish

ADULT SIZE
female 2 ³/₄ in (7cm)
male 3 in (8cm)

DIET
all foods

EASE OF KEEPING
10/10

PH RANGE
6.8–7.5

This species, also known as BA tetras, are beautiful fish with a black bar through the body and oranges and reds in their fins. However, they can be aggressive towards fish that are slightly larger than they are and also to smaller fish, which can be a problem. They will also chew and destroy fine-leafed plants and thus require hardy plants in the aquarium, such as umbrella fern, giant twisted vallis or Amazon swords. They are very easy to breed but are voracious in finding and eating the eggs after they have spawned. They will typically group spawn, with the eggs being showered everywhere. The eggs, if you can save them, are easy to hatch and the fry will readily will grow on to become adults.

Feeding
They will take all types of food, but thrive on a wide variety of flakes, frozen and live foods. They will be one of the first to feed when food is placed in the tank. Be careful not to overfeed.

Garnet or Pretty Tetra / *Hemigrammus pulcher*

This is a fish that has been known for many years but has only recently been imported in any quantities. With flashes of red around the eye, and black and gold at the rear end of its body with silver scaling, this fish is an absolute delight to keep in the aquarium. Keep a shoal of them together in a well-planted tank and they will do exceptionally well. They will mix with anything. If they have a problem, it is because they are so timid. Having plenty of plants in the aquarium will help immensely as they will have somewhere to dive into for cover.

Feeding

They will take all types of food, but thrive on a wide variety of flakes, frozen and live foods. Make sure that their food is broken down small enough for them to eat.

ORIGIN
south america

TEMPERATURE RANGE
73–79°F (23–26°C)

COMMUNITY
excellent

ADULT SIZE
female 2 $\frac{1}{2}$ in (6.5cm)
male 2 $\frac{1}{2}$ in (6.5cm)

DIET
all foods

EASE OF KEEPING
8/10

PH RANGE
6.8–7.5

Gold Tetra / *Hemigrammus armstrongi*

ORIGIN
south america

TEMPERATURE RANGE
73–79°F (23–26°C)

COMMUNITY
very good

ADULT SIZE
female 2 in (5cm)
male 2 in (5cm)

DIET
all foods

EASE OF KEEPING
8/10

PH RANGE
6.8–7.5

As you can see from the picture this fish has a gold sheen all over its body. When there is a group of them moving about the aquarium they tend to swim quite quickly and are forever turning in the light. This gives a beautiful effect of gold flashing all over the aquarium. If there are only one or two in a tank they can chase other fish about but if they are in a shoal, they will chase within their own group. Plenty of fine-leafed plants are required in the aquarium for them. They are very easy to breed but will look for their eggs and eat them. There is no parental care for the eggs at all. The fry are quite easy to grow on if you spawn the adults in a special tank and are able to keep the eggs. They are very hardy and are ideal for the new aquarium.

Feeding
They will take all types of food, but thrive on a wide variety of flakes, frozen and live foods. They will be one of the first to feed when food is placed in the tank. Be careful not to overfeed.

Marginatus Pencilfish / *Nannobrycon marginatus*

This is a delightful, peaceful little fish. They are very easy to care for but they do require good quality water conditions. If you use plenty of plants such as cabomba and bogmoss you may well find that they will spawn without any prompting. They scatter their eggs within the plant leaves and the eggs will then stick to them. There is no parental care but they do not eat their eggs. The fry need exceptionally small food, such as microsorium to start with, but once they are over the first few days, normally they will grow on without a problem.

ORIGIN
south america

TEMPERATURE RANGE
73–79°F (23–26°C)

COMMUNITY
excellent

ADULT SIZE
female 1 ½ in (4cm)
male 1 ½ in (4cm)

DIET
all foods

EASE OF KEEPING
8/10

PH RANGE
6.8–7.5

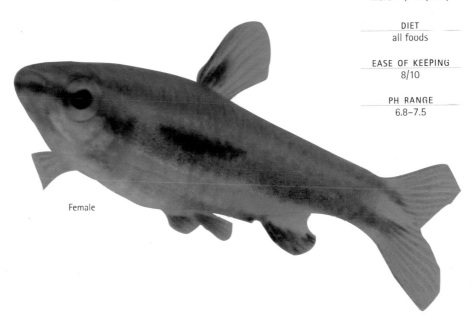

Female

Male

Feeding

They will take all types of food, but thrive on a wide variety of flakes, frozen and live foods. Make sure that their food is broken down small enough for them to eat. Break the larger food down by rubbing it between your fingers.

Paraguay Tetra / *Aphyocharax paraguayensis*

As the name suggests, these fish originate from Paraguay and not many fish are exported from there. However, breeders in the Far East now breed them in quite large quantities so they are easily available to us. These fish are best kept with larger tetras as they will chase and harass smaller fish. If they start doing this, they will progress to nipping the fins of the smaller fish. Paraguay tetra have a lovely silvery sheen over the body, and jet-black markings in the anal fin and caudal peduncle area complement this. They are easy to keep and breed and are hardy enough to be one of the first fish you place into your aquarium.

Feeding

They will take all types of food, but thrive on a wide variety of flakes, frozen and live foods. They will be one of the first to feed when food is placed in the tank. Be careful not to overfeed.

ORIGIN
south america

TEMPERATURE RANGE
73–79°F (23–26°C)

COMMUNITY
good

ADULT SIZE
female 2 ½ (6.5cm)
male 2 ½ in (6.5cm)

DIET
all foods

EASE OF KEEPING
9/10

PH RANGE
6.8–7.5

TETRA

Half Line Hemiodus / *Hemiodopsis microlepis*

ORIGIN
south america

TEMPERATURE RANGE
71.5–82°F (22–28°C)

COMMUNITY
good with larger fish

ADULT SIZE
female 6 ¼ in (16cm)
male 6 ¼ in (16cm)

DIET
all foods

EASE OF KEEPING
9/10

PH RANGE
6.8–7.2

There are about 16 of the Hemiodus family all called Half Line Hemiodus, the main difference being the patterning in the rear half of the body, but this can sometimes be difficult to see. Some have solid lines while in others, like this one, the line is made up of blotches. Breeding habits of this fish are unknown and it is also extremely difficult to tell the difference between male and female. For their size they can be a very timid fish and like plenty of plant cover in the aquarium. They will go after very small fish and so it is advisable to only keep them with larger fish.

Feeding

They will take all types of food, but thrive on a wide variety of flakes, frozen and live foods. They will be one of the first to feed when food is placed in the tank. Be careful not to overfeed.

Three Striped or Brown Tailed Pencilfish /
Nannobrycon eques

As with all of the pencil fish, they are extremely peaceful. They have very simple requirements such as plenty of plants to hide and rest in and a good variety of foods. This fish is quite easy to breed in exactly the same way as the Marginatus pencilfish. They are best kept in a shoal of 10–12. They swim in a rather unusual way, in as much as they swim tail down at an angle of about 30 degrees. This is quite normal, so do not worry when you see this happen.

Feeding
They will take all types of food, but thrive on a wide variety of flakes, frozen and live foods. Make sure that their food is broken down small enough for them to eat.

ORIGIN
south america

TEMPERATURE RANGE
73–79°F (23–26°C)

COMMUNITY
excellent

ADULT SIZE
female 1 ³/₄ in (4.5cm)
male 1 ³/₄ in (4.5cm)

DIET
all foods

EASE OF KEEPING
9/10

PH RANGE
6.8–7.0

TETRA

Sawbwa Tetra / *Sawbwa resplendens*

ORIGIN
southern asia

TEMPERATURE RANGE
70–77°F (21–25°C)

COMMUNITY
very good

ADULT SIZE
female 1 ¹/₂ in (4cm)
male 1 ¹/₂ in (4cm)

DIET
all foods

EASE OF KEEPING
9/10

PH RANGE
6.8–7.0

This fish is not a tetra but a rasbora. It has only been known to the hobby for about 10 years and was originally grouped in with the tetras. However, further investigations have been done on this fish and it is now known to be a rasbora, although hobbyists still call it a tetra. As it matures, the whole of the snout area of its head becomes bright red. The body is semi-translucent so you can see the backbone of the fish. There are black markings on the dorsal and red ends to the lobes of the tail. The fish prefers to be in a shoal and is very easy to keep.

Feeding

They will take all types of food, but thrive on a wide variety of flakes, frozen and live foods. Make sure that their food is broken down small enough for them to eat.

Silver Dollar / *Mylossoma argenteum*

This fish is quite hardy and easy to keep. They prefer plants in the aquarium such as straight vallis, rushes and any other tall plants that they can swim through. Although they will eat your plants, if you feed them sufficient vegetable foods this will not happen. There is no information as to the breeding or sexing of this fish. Generally, if they are bought when they are small and kept with smaller fish, as long as they are well fed, there is normally no problem with the smaller fish. They can be kept as single fish but look better if there are two or three in the aquarium.

Feeding

They will take all types of food, but do much better when fed foods such as lettuce, peas and spirulina.

ORIGIN
south america

TEMPERATURE RANGE
73–79°F (23–26°C)

COMMUNITY
good with larger fish
only

ADULT SIZE
female 6 in (15cm)
male 6 in (15cm)

DIET
mostly vegetable foods

EASE OF KEEPING
9/10

PH RANGE
6.8–7.0

TETRA

Black Banded Pyrrhulina / *Copella cf. nigrofasciata*

ORIGIN
south america

TEMPERATURE RANGE
70-77°C (21-25°C)

COMMUNITY
excellent

ADULT SIZE
female 2 ¹/₂ in (6.5cm)
male 2 ¹/₂ in (6.5cm)

DIET
all foods

EASE OF KEEPING
7/10

PH RANGE
6.8-7.0

With bright red dots all of the way down the length of the body and a black bar behind that runs right the way through the eye, this a very attractive little fish. When first imported, they always look as though they are starved of food but this is just the way they are. It is not until they start to mature that their body starts to fill out and colour up. They can be a little difficult to maintain but this is generally due to not being given a good variety of quality foods. They relish live brine shrimp and young live daphnia. They will tend to hide away for the first couple of months but once they have established themselves you will see them quite happily swimming around the aquarium.

Feeding

They will take all types of food, but thrive on a wide variety of flakes, frozen and live foods. Make sure that their food is broken down small enough for them to eat.

TETRA

Spotted Splash Tetra / *Pyrrhulina sp.*

ORIGIN
south america

TEMPERATURE RANGE
70–75°F (21–24°C)

COMMUNITY
excellent

ADULT SIZE
female 2 ¹/₂ in (6.5cm)
male 2 ¹/₂ in (6.5cm)

DIET
all foods

EASE OF KEEPING
8/10

PH RANGE
6.8–7.0

As with most splash tetras, this variety is not imported as a specific fish but is found in and amongst the boxes of other fish. They typically arrive with other fish from Surinam, Guyana, Colombia and Brazil. Again, my experience has shown that they prefer to be in a small shoal but are total community fish. This particular one has a silvery white body with five rows of black dots along the length of the body and lemon and black tipped fins. They always seem very bright and alert with fins erect and are always looking for food. They normally feed in the top half of the aquarium, so do not feed too much sinking food.

Feeding

They will take all types of food, but thrive on a wide variety of flakes, frozen and live foods. Make sure that their food is broken down small enough for them to eat.

Red Splash Tetra / *Pyrrhulina sp.*

When this fish is newly imported, they are always very skinny and exceptionally nervous. They require an aquarium that has plenty of plant cover for them to hide away in. They need to be fed regularly, probably more than usual, but only with food that is rich in vitamins and also plenty of varied live food. They will take some time to fill out but when they do, they get a nice thick and deep body. They are better kept in a small shoal of five or more. They have beautiful red fins with jet-black edging and a lovely red tail. They will take time to settle in your aquarium but are well worth the wait.

Feeding

They will take all types of food, but thrive on a wide variety of flakes, frozen and live foods. Make sure that their food is broken down small enough for them to eat.

ORIGIN
south america

TEMPERATURE RANGE
68–75°F (20–24°C)

COMMUNITY
excellent

ADULT SIZE
female 2 ³/₄ in (7cm)
male 2 ³/₄ in (7cm)

DIET
all foods

EASE OF KEEPING
8/10

PH RANGE
6.8–7.0

Redback Bleeding Heart Tetra /
Hyphessobrycon pyrrhonotus

ORIGIN
south america

TEMPERATURE RANGE
75–82°F (24–28°C)

COMMUNITY
excellent

ADULT SIZE
female 2 ¹/₄ (6cm)
male 2 ¹/₄ in (6cm)

DIET
all foods

EASE OF KEEPING
9/10

PH RANGE
6.5–7.0

This is a very close relative of the standard Bleeding Heart tetra. The lower half of the body has reflective silvery scales and the upper half has reflective red scaling. Telling the difference between male and female is quite easy. The male has an extended, pointed dorsal fin, while in the female, the dorsal is shorter and rounded. The female will also get very plump in the body when well fed and ready to spawn. They will just scatter the eggs and then go hunting for them.

Feeding
They will take all types of food, but thrive on a wide variety of flakes, frozen and live foods. Make sure that their food is broken down small enough for them to eat.

Red Three Lined Pencilfish /
Nannostomus trifasciatus "Red"

This is a very new fish to the hobby and because of their price they are not seen in many aquarium shops. They are quite expensive for their size but it is well worth buying four or five for their colour. The body has a deep red hue all over with the lines showing through and the fins are a very strong red. When first imported, you will only see them at about $^1/_2$–1 in (2–3cm) long. Once you have them feeding and they are settled in your aquarium they will fill out and show their colouration very quickly. They do much better in a well-planted aquarium.

Feeding

They will take all types of food, but thrive on a wide variety of flakes, frozen and live foods. Make sure that their food is broken down small enough for them to eat.

ORIGIN
south america

TEMPERATURE RANGE
70–77°F (21–25°C)

COMMUNITY
excellent

ADULT SIZE
female 1 $^1/_2$ in (4cm)
male 1 $^1/_2$ in (4cm)

DIET
all foods

EASE OF KEEPING
8/10

PH RANGE
6..5–7.0

BARBS

Albino Tiger Barb / *Barbus tetrazona Albino*

ORIGIN
asia

TEMPERATURE RANGE
71.5–79°F (22–26°C)

COMMUNITY
good

ADULT SIZE
female 2 ³/₄ in (7cm)
male 2 ³/₄ in (7cm)

DIET
all foods

EASE OF KEEPING
9/10

pH RANGE
6.8–7.5

The Albino Tiger barb is as boisterous as the standard Tiger barb. They are fine if kept in a small shoal and will chase amongst themselves. If kept in only ones or twos they can become fin nippers. The albino has lovely highlighted metallic scales, which are quite random over the upper half of the body so no two fish are identical. Breeding is quite easy but, as with other albino fish, pairing two together will not give you 100 per cent albino. Quite a high percentage will revert to their original genetic colouring.

Feeding

They will take all types of food, but thrive on a wide variety of flakes, frozen and live foods. They will be one of the first to feed when food is placed in the tank. So ensure that there is plenty of food for the other fish in your aquarium without overfeeding and polluting your tank.

Arulius or Longfin Barb / *Barbus arulius*

For a barb that grows to 5 in (13cm) as an adult, this is a very good community fish. It has no natural enemies in the wild and so has naturally become very docile and tolerant towards other fish, even those that are much smaller. The picture shown is of a female. The male is easy to distinguish because it is generally much slimmer than the female, the dorsal fin has elongated fin rays and it is a much stronger colour. They prefer to be in a large aquarium with plenty of broad-leafed plants.

Feeding

They will take all types of food, but thrive on a wide variety of flakes, frozen and live foods. They will be one of the first to feed when food is placed in the tank. Be careful not to overfeed.

ORIGIN
india (asia)

TEMPERATURE RANGE
68–79°F (20–26°C)

COMMUNITY
very good

ADULT SIZE
female 5 in (13cm)
male 5 in (13cm)

DIET
all foods

EASE OF KEEPING
9/10

PH RANGE
6.5–7.0

Albino Red Tailed Tinfoil Barb /
Barbus schwanenfeldi Albino

ORIGIN
south east asia

TEMPERATURE RANGE
71.5–79°F (22–26°C)

COMMUNITY
larger community fish
only

ADULT SIZE
female 13 ¹/₂ in (35cm)
male 13 ¹/₂ in (35cm)

DIET
all foods

EASE OF KEEPING
9/10

PH RANGE
6.8–7.5

This is a fish that needs to be in with larger fish. This is not because they are aggressive but because they grow so large. They need an aquarium larger than 48 in (122cm) to grow to their best. Light planting with giant straight vallis or long flowing onion plants will make these fish feel very much at home. They grow very quickly. Normally available in a shop at about 2 in (5cm), you can expect them to grow to about 6 in (15cm) within the first year.

Feeding

They will take all types of food, but thrive on a wide variety of flakes, frozen and live foods. They will be one of the first to feed when food is placed in the tank. Larger foods such as chopped earthworm or mealworms will be taken quite readily but only feed as part of their main diet.

Black Ruby Barb / *Barbus nigrofasciatus*

Although similar to the Tiger barbs, the Black Ruby is a much quieter fish in the aquarium. They are quite happy if they are on their own but look much better if there is a shoal of them. The males will also colour up much more strongly if they are vying for the attention of the females. A male in good condition or in breeding colours has a strong red hue all over its body, very strong black bars running top to bottom and a jet black dorsal fin. The female is somewhat plainer in colouration and much plumper.

Feeding

They will take all types of food, but thrive on a wide variety of flakes, frozen and live foods. They will be one of the first to feed when food is placed in the tank. Be careful not to overfeed.

ORIGIN
asia

TEMPERATURE RANGE
71.5–79°F (22–26°C)

COMMUNITY
very good

ADULT SIZE
female 2 $\frac{1}{2}$ in (6.5cm)
male 2 $\frac{1}{2}$ in (6.5cm)

DIET
all foods

EASE OF KEEPING
10/10

PH RANGE
6.8–7.2

BARB

Clown Barb / *Barbus everetti*

ORIGIN
borneo (asia)

TEMPERATURE RANGE
73–79°F (23–26°C)

COMMUNITY
very good

ADULT SIZE
female 4 in (10cm)
male 4 in (10cm)

DIET
all foods

EASE OF KEEPING
9/10

PH RANGE
6.8–7.2

Although, again one of the larger barbs, as with the Arulius barb this is a total community fish. They can be mixed with just about anything. Normally available in an aquarium shop at about 1 in (2.5cm), they are quite long lived fish and are also slow growing. They will take three to four years to attain their maximum length. They are not happy being moved about too much and in the early days are susceptible to fungal problems. However, normally, once you have cured this they should settle down nicely and give no further problems.

Feeding

They will take all types of food, but thrive on a wide variety of flakes, frozen and live foods. They will be one of the first to feed when food is placed in the tank. Be careful not to overfeed.

Ember or Banded Barb /
Barbus fasciatus (B. melanympyx)

As with many of the barbs, they do not like being moved about and quite often have disease problems when first imported. This variety is no different and has a susceptibility to white spot, which can be difficult to treat. A combination of higher temperature and medication is usually the answer to this and, once settled, they should have no further problems. They like a well-planted aquarium with plants such as cabomba, hairgrass and moneywort. Breeding this fish is not always easy, although it is very simple to tell the difference between male and female because of the colouration.

ORIGIN
asia

TEMPERATURE RANGE
71.5–79°F (22–26°C)

COMMUNITY
very good

ADULT SIZE
female 2 ³/₄ (7cm)
male 2 ³/₄ in (7cm)

DIET
all foods

EASE OF KEEPING
9/10

PH RANGE
6.8–7.5

Feeding

They will take all types of food, but thrive on a
wide variety of flakes, frozen and live foods. They
will be one of the first to feed when food is
placed in the tank once they have settled into
their new aquarium. Be careful not to overfeed.

Golden Dwarf Barb / *Barbus gelius*

A shoal of these fish in your aquarium is a delight to watch. They swim with all of their fins erect and are always moving slowly around the aquarium. As you can see from the picture, the upper half of the body is golden with black blotches. When seen in the aquarium shop, they are normally passed by because they are so small and the colouration has not set in yet. They prefer to have plenty of plant cover to hide in. When that happens, they will dart for cover but very soon come back out into the open areas of your aquarium.

Feeding
They will take all types of food, but thrive on a wide variety of flakes, frozen and live foods. Make sure that their food is broken down small enough for them to eat.

ORIGIN
zaire (africa)

TEMPERATURE RANGE
66–75°F (19–24°C)

COMMUNITY
excellent

ADULT SIZE
female 1 ¹/₂ in (4cm)
male 1 ¹/₂ in (4cm)

DIET
all foods

EASE OF KEEPING
10/10

PH RANGE
6.8 – 7.2

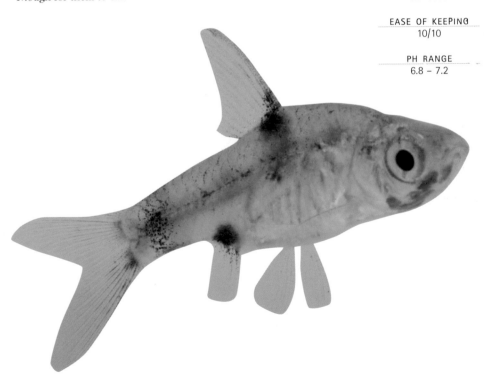

BARB

Ghost Tiger Barb / *Barbus tetrazona Ghost*

ORIGIN
asia

TEMPERATURE RANGE
71.5–79°F (22–26°C)

COMMUNITY
good

ADULT SIZE
female 2 ³/₄ in (7cm)
male 2 ³/₄ in (7cm)

DIET
all foods

EASE OF KEEPING
9/10

PH RANGE
6.8–7.5

This variety is very similar to the standard Tiger barb and can easily be mistaken for them. The main difference is that this fish has a semi-translucent body where you can see some of its spine and insides. Many of the varieties of Tiger barb that we see are actually found in the wild, but only in exceptionally small numbers because a problem has occurred in the breeding and the colouration is genetically wrong. However, commercial breeders in the Far East have been encouraged by fish-keepers to breed them in greater numbers because the breed has become quite popular.

Feeding

They will take all types of food, but thrive on a wide variety of flakes, frozen and live foods. They will be one of the first to feed when food is placed in the tank. Be careful not to overfeed.

Red Tailed Tinfoil Barb / *Barbus schwanenfeldi*

As with the albino variety of this fish, they should be kept with larger fish only. Again it is not because they are aggressive but because they grow so large. They also need an aquarium larger than 48 in (122cm) to grow to their best. Light planting with giant straight vallis or long flowing onion plant will make them feel very much at home and they will grow very quickly. They are normally available in an aquarium shop at about 2 in (5cm), but you can expect them to grow to about 6 in (15cm) within the first year.

Feeding

They will take all types of food, but thrive on a wide variety of flakes, frozen and live foods. They will be one of the first to feed when food is placed in the tank. Larger foods such as chopped earthworms or mealworms will be taken quite readily but only feed as part of their diet.

ORIGIN
south east asia

TEMPERATURE RANGE
71.5–79°F (22–26°C)

COMMUNITY
larger community fish only

ADULT SIZE
female 13 1/2 in (35cm)
male 13 1/2 in (35cm)

DIET
all foods

EASE OF KEEPING
9/10

PH RANGE
6.8–7.5

BARB

Striped or Lined Barb / *Barbus lineatus*

ORIGIN
zaire (africa)

TEMPERATURE RANGE
70–77°F (21–25°C)

COMMUNITY
very good

ADULT SIZE
female 4 ¹/₄ in (11cm)
male 4 ¹/₄ in (11cm)

DIET
all foods

EASE OF KEEPING
10/10

PH RANGE
6.8–7.5

The elongated shape of this fish tells you that it is a very fast and strong swimmer. It is found in fast flowing rivers or streams in Zaire. When it needs to rest, it will find a place behind a rock or sunken log, where the current will not affect it, and stay there until it regains its energy. With its golden hue and black lines the length of its body and yellowy fins, you can see that it is a striking fish. Do not it put in with really small fish as it is liable to be bullied out of the way and may get damaged.

Feeding

They will take all types of food, but thrive on a wide variety of flakes, frozen and live foods. They will be one of the first to feed when food is placed in the tank. Be careful not to overfeed.

Striped Flying Barb / *Esomus lineatus*

Unfortunately, we do not see this fish very often in aquarium shops as they are rather difficult obtain. However, when we do see them, they always seem to be in excellent condition and have been found to be a very hardy fish to keep. You will need to keep a tight-fitting lid on your aquarium as they jump out of the water. The pectoral fins on this fish are very large and they give the fish the power to push itself out of the water. It is a very pretty fish with subtle colouration and is a delight to keep.

Feeding

They will take all types of food, but thrive on a wide variety of flakes, frozen and live foods. They will be one of the first to feed when food is placed in the tank. Be careful not to overfeed. They will also jump out of the water when feeding from the surface.

ORIGIN
india (asia)

TEMPERATURE RANGE
71.5–77°F (22–25°C)

COMMUNITY
excellent

ADULT SIZE
female 2 $\frac{1}{4}$ in (6cm)
male 2 $\frac{1}{4}$ in (6cm)

DIET
all foods

EASE OF KEEPING
10/10

PH RANGE
6.8–7.2

BARB

Albino Cherry Barb / *Barbus titteya Albino*

ORIGIN
asia

TEMPERATURE RANGE
71.5–79°F (22–26°C)

COMMUNITY
excellent

ADULT SIZE
female 1 ³/₄ in (4.5cm)
male 1 ³/₄ in (4.5cm)

DIET
all foods

EASE OF KEEPING
10/10

PH RANGE
6.8–7.5

The albino variety of the Cherry barb is quite rare and although they are bred commercially in the Far East they are only bred in very small numbers. This makes them quite expensive to buy. Being an albino and also quite a small fish, they need plenty of plant cover in the aquarium but they do not hide away all the time. They use the plants mainly to give them confidence in their surroundings. They have beautiful red eyes and a reflective gold line in the upper part of their body that makes them really stand out in your aquarium. A very worthwhile purchase.

Feeding
They will take all types of food, but thrive on a wide variety of flakes, frozen and live foods. Make sure that their food is broken down small enough for them to eat.

Denisoni Barb / *Barbus denisonii*

The only problem with this fish is that it demands very high quality water conditions. If there is a problem with the water, it will suffer very quickly and very badly. If the conditions are good, it will thrive. With its red, black and yellow markings this fish looks quite outstanding in any aquarium. The only problem is that they are quite expensive and may cost between £12–20 depending on the size. This variety is quite a recent addition to the trade and is very sought after. It is a very fast swimmer, so if you need to catch this fish, use an over-sized, soft net so that you do not damage it.

Feeding

They will take all types of food, but thrive on a wide variety of flakes, frozen and live foods. They will be one of the first to feed when food is placed in the tank. Be careful not to overfeed.

ORIGIN
india (asia)

TEMPERATURE RANGE
68–77°F (20–25°C)

COMMUNITY
excellent

ADULT SIZE
female 5 ³/₄ in (15cm)
male 5 ³/₄ in (15cm)

DIET
all foods

EASE OF KEEPING
9/10

PH RANGE
6.8 – 7.2

Amiets Killie / *Aphyosemion amietii*

ORIGIN
africa

TEMPERATURE RANGE
71.5–80.5°F (22–27°C)

COMMUNITY
excellent

ADULT SIZE
female 2 $\frac{1}{4}$ in (6cm)
male 2 $\frac{3}{4}$ in (7cm)

DIET
all foods

EASE OF KEEPING
9/10

PH RANGE
6.8–7.2

As with most killifish, the males are far more colourful than the females. The females have relatively few markings or colours. However, where this variety is concerned the female has yellow fins and spotting in the body. The males are generally very dominant and can bully the females around the aquarium. There is a fallacy that killifish are difficult to keep but that is generally because they have a short lifespan. In the wild, many of this type of fish will live for less than a year, but that is as a result of the environment in which they live. When the annual drought is over and there is water in the ponds or streams where they live, they will hatch out, grow into adults, spawn a new crop of eggs and then die because

Male

the water dries out. When the rains come again, the eggs are triggered and hatch out and so the cycle goes on. In your aquarium, because the water does not dry out, you can expect a much longer lifespan.

Feeding

They will take all types of food, but thrive on a wide variety of flakes, frozen and live foods. Young daphnia and brine shrimp are ideal food for these fish, especially to get them into breeding condition. Make sure that their food is broken down small enough for them to eat.

Female

Sparkling Panchax / *Aplochielus lineatus Gold*

ORIGIN
africa

TEMPERATURE RANGE
71.5–80.5°F (22–27°C)

COMMUNITY
excellent

ADULT SIZE
female 3 in (8cm)
male 3 ¹/₂ in (9cm)

DIET
all foods

EASE OF KEEPING
10/10

PH RANGE
6.8–7.2

This killifish is a surface feeder. It has a slightly upturned mouth, which is ideal for taking small insects from the surface of the water in the wild. The male has reflective scales with a golden body, yellow fins and a red edging to the upper and lower lobes of the tail. The female has a plain body with orange to red edges to the tail and anal fin. Plenty of fine plants are required in your aquarium for these fish, as they will breed in amongst the fine leaves to which the eggs attach. If you wish to breed these fish, it is best to do so in a small separate tank, specially set up for them.

Male

Feeding
They will take all types of food, but thrive on a wide variety of flakes, frozen and live foods. Make sure that their food is broken down small enough for them to eat.

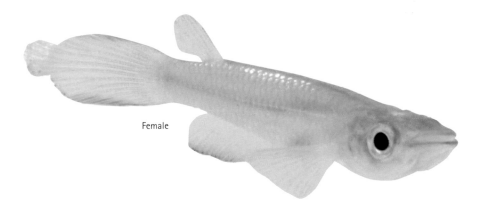

Female

Normans Lampeye / *Aplochielichthys normani*

ORIGIN
west africa

TEMPERATURE RANGE
71.5–80.5°F (22–27°C)

COMMUNITY
excellent

ADULT SIZE
female 1 in (3cm)
male 1 ¹/₂ in (4cm)

DIET
all foods

EASE OF KEEPING
9/10

PH RANGE
6.8–7.2

Lampeyes are generally quite hardy and very easy to keep and breed. Because of their smallness at adult size, they can be lost within an aquarium and so to get a good display you would need to have a shoal numbering 20 or more. Luckily they are very cheap to buy from an aquarium shop but, even better, they are very easy to breed. The males have longer and more pointed fins than the females so they are very easy to sex. They will spawn in amongst plants with very fine leaves and then leave the eggs to hatch out on their own.

Feeding
They will take all types of food, but thrive on a wide variety of flakes, frozen and live foods. Make sure that their food is broken down small enough for them to eat.

Gunthers Notho / *Nothobranchius guentheri Gold*

When buying these beautiful fish, try to buy them in threes, one male and two females. This is because when the male decides that he wants to breed, he will drive the female hard. If there is more than one female available, his attentions will be shared between them and it will not be so difficult for either of them. Having more females is even better. They like to dive into a peat substrate with the female shedding the eggs and the male fertilising them. Their eggs are then left to their own devices with no parental care at all. *N. geuntheri* has a number of colour varieties of which this is one.

ORIGIN
africa

TEMPERATURE RANGE
71.5–77°F (22–25°C)

COMMUNITY
excellent

ADULT SIZE
female 1 ³/₄ in (4.5cm)
male 1 ³/₄ in (4.5cm)

DIET
all foods

EASE OF KEEPING
9/10

PH RANGE
6.8–7.2

male

Feeding

They will take all types of food, but thrive on a wide variety of flakes, frozen and live foods. Make sure that their food is broken down small enough for them to eat. Live foods such as bloodworm, daphnia, glassworm and tubifex are very good for these fish.

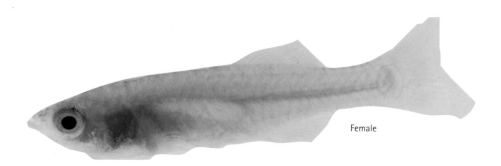

Female

Korthaus' Notho / *Nothobranchius korthause*

As with all other Nothobranchius species, they are collectively known as 'peat divers'. This is because of their habit of diving into a muddy or peat substrate to spawn. This can be very easily set up by using an old, clean plastic butter container and cutting a hole about 2 in (5cm) square in the lid. Buy some Irish peat moss and boil enough to fill the container. When it has boiled, drain it into another container and allow it to cool completely. Put a small amount of gravel into the base of the butter dish to weigh it down and then fill with the peat moss. Very carefully place this on the substrate of your aquarium and the fish will find it when they are ready.

Feeding

They will take all types of food, but thrive on a wide variety of flakes, frozen and live foods. Make sure that their food is broken down small enough for them to eat. Live foods such as bloodworm, daphnia, glassworm and tubifex are very good for these fish.

ORIGIN
africa

TEMPERATURE RANGE
71.5–79°F (22–26°C)

COMMUNITY
excellent

ADULT SIZE
female 1 ³/₄ in (4.5cm)
male 2 in (5cm)

DIET
all foods

EASE OF KEEPING
9/10

PH RANGE
6.8–7.2

Male

Female

Feeding

They will take all types of food, but thrive on a wide variety of flakes, frozen and live foods. Make sure that their food is broken down small enough for them to eat. Live foods such as bloodworm, daphnia, glassworm and tubifex are very good for these fish.

Red Finned Notho / *Nothobranchius rubripinnis*

The colouration of the entire Nothobranchius group is quite vivid. With bright reds, yellows and blues being the main colours, they will make very popular additions to your aquarium. Most of these fish are bred and supplied by private breeders and one of the main countries for this is the Czech Republic. The breeders there specialise in breeding and growing just a few varieties so that they can give them all their attention. This way, better quality stock is available.

ORIGIN
tanzania (africa)

TEMPERATURE RANGE
73–82°F (23–28°C)

COMMUNITY
excellent

ADULT SIZE
female 1 ³/₄ in (4.5cm)
male 2 in (5cm)

DIET
all foods

EASE OF KEEPING
9/10

PH RANGE
6.8–7.2

Male

Female

Feeding
They will take all types of food, but thrive on a wide variety of flakes, frozen and live foods. Make sure that their food is broken down small enough for them to eat. Live foods such as bloodworm, daphnia, glassworm and tubifex are very good for these fish.

Dangila Danio / *Danio dangila*

One of the larger danios growing to about 6 in (15cm), they are normally available in the aquarium shop at about 2 in (5cm). They are quite a slow growing fish and require a good-sized aquarium but they are very easy to keep. The front half of the body is plain, with the rear half made up of broken lines that continue through to the end of the tail. The dorsal and anal fins are a very subtle lemon colour. The female is much deeper in the belly area than the male. They do not need to be kept in a shoal but will look better this way.

Feeding

They will take all types of food, but thrive on a wide variety of flakes, frozen and live foods. They will be one of the first to feed when food is placed in the tank. Be careful not to overfeed.

ORIGIN
india (asia)

TEMPERATURE RANGE
70–77°F (21–25°C)

COMMUNITY
very good

ADULT SIZE
female 4 in (10cm)
male 4 in (10cm)

DIET
all foods

EASE OF KEEPING
9/10

PH RANGE
6.8–7.5

Bengal Danio / *Danio devario*

ORIGIN
asia

TEMPERATURE RANGE
68--77°F (20-25°C)

COMMUNITY
very good

ADULT SIZE
female 5 ³/₄ in (15cm)
male 5 ³/₄ in (15cm)

DIET
all foods

EASE OF KEEPING
9/10

PH RANGE
6.8-7.5

As with all of the danios, this is another very hardy fish. They are ideal fish to put into your aquarium when you first set it up. They will swim at all levels but predominantly in the upper half. Their mouth is slightly upturned so they will mainly feed from the surface but if they are given live food, such as daphnia, in the lower half of the aquarium, they will swim after it without hesitation. The male has a much slimmer and shallower body than the female. They are egg scatterers, and once they have spawned will go looking for the eggs and eat them.

Feeding

They will take all types of food, but thrive on a wide variety of flakes, frozen and live foods. They will be one of the first to feed when food is placed in the tank. Be careful not to overfeed.

Glowlight Danio / *Danio choprae*

This danio has been known for a long time but it is only in the last couple of years that it has come to prominence. They do exceptionally well if kept in a shoal of 10 or more. The colouration of this fish will be enhanced by good and varied lighting in the aquarium. The males are much slimmer than the females but when spawning they drive the females very hard. They also like plenty of plants in the aquarium to swim amongst. They are quite expensive because they are quite rare but they are well worth the cost. They are ideal fish for the beginner both to keep and breed.

Feeding

They will take all types of food, but thrive on a wide variety of flakes, frozen and live foods. They will be one of the first to feed when food is placed in the tank. Be careful not to overfeed.

ORIGIN
asia

TEMPERATURE RANGE
64–77°F (18–25°C)

COMMUNITY
excellent

ADULT SIZE
female 1 in (3cm)
male 1 in (3cm)

DIET
all foods

EASE OF KEEPING
10/10

PH RANGE
6.8–7.5

Blue Paradise Fish / *Macropodus opercularis*

ORIGIN
asia

TEMPERATURE RANGE
71.5–80.5°F (22–27°C)

COMMUNITY
very good

ADULT SIZE
female 3 ¹/₂ in (9cm)
male 3 ¹/₂ in (9cm)

DIET
all foods

EASE OF KEEPING
9/10

PH RANGE
6.8–7.5

The anabantoid or gourami group of fish are generally very easy to keep. This blue variety of the Paradise fish is no different. Placing two males together in your aquarium will normally make them show off to each other and their colouration and finnage will become enhanced. The females have shorter fins and are much fuller in the body than the males. They prefer fine-leafed plants in the aquarium as they are bubble-nest breeders and use small bits of the plant to bind their nest together.

Feeding
They will take all types of food, but thrive on a wide variety of flakes, frozen and live foods. Live foods such as bloodworm, daphnia, glassworm and tubifex are very good for these fish.

Chocolate Gourami / *Sphaerichthys osphromenoides*

Although this is a very sought after fish, it is rarely seen in aquarium shops because it can be very difficult to settle in when first imported. They have to be looked after very carefully, and understandably many aquarium shops are aware of this problem. In defence of the fish, once they are settled, they generally are no problem and are a pleasure to keep and grow on. They have a habit of swimming around with their fins tightly clamped and so this is not to be seen as a problem with the fish. They are mouthbrooders and so are quite a challenge for the fish-keeper to breed.

Feeding

They will take all types of food, but thrive on a wide variety of flakes, frozen and live foods. Make sure that their food is broken down small enough for them to eat. Live foods such as bloodworm, daphnia, glassworm and tubifex are very good for these fish.

ORIGIN
asia

TEMPERATURE RANGE
73–85°F (23–29°C)

COMMUNITY
excellent

ADULT SIZE
female 2 in (5cm)
male 2 in (5cm)

DIET
all foods

EASE OF KEEPING
6/10

PH RANGE
6.5–7.0

Croaking Gourami / *Trichopsis vittata*

ORIGIN
asia

TEMPERATURE RANGE
71.5–80.5°F (22–27°C)

COMMUNITY
excellent

ADULT SIZE
female 2 in (5cm)
male 2 in (5cm)

DIET
all foods

EASE OF KEEPING
10/10

PH RANGE
6.8–7.5

As with all of the gouramies, they are air breathers. When they are swimming in the aquarium you will see them release a small bubble of air and then a minute or two later, they will swim up to the surface and replenish their air supply before diving back down again. The male has a much longer pointed anal fin than the female. To breed these fish, the temperature has to be raised by about 5-6° and so they need to be in a separate small aquarium to do this. The fry, when they hatch out, are very small and need micro food.

Feeding

They will take all types of food, but thrive on a wide variety of flakes, frozen and live foods. Make sure that their food is broken down small enough for them to eat. Live foods such as bloodworm, daphnia, glassworm and tubifex are very good for these fish.

Green Kissing Gourami / *Helostomma temminckii*

The Kissing gouramies can and do grow very large. Fortunately, in most home aquariums they will only grow to about 6 in (15cm). For a potentially large fish, they are quite slow growing. They will enjoy any soft plants that you have in your aquarium. The habit of two fish 'kissing' is in fact a way of testing each other's strength. They do not damage themselves or the other fish but they will bully their way around your aquarium. The photograph shows the wild form but there is also a pink and a marbled variety.

ORIGIN
asia

TEMPERATURE RANGE
71.5–79°F (22–26°C)

COMMUNITY
good

ADULT SIZE
female 12 in (30cm)
male 12 in (30cm)

DIET
vegetable foods as
main diet

EASE OF KEEPING
9/10

PH RANGE
6.8–7.5

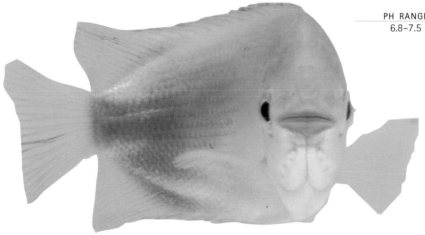

Feeding
They will take all types of food, but thrive on a wide variety of flake and frozen foods that are made up mainly of vegetable matter such as spirulina, lettuce leaves and boiled peas. Algae tablets are also another good food as part of their diet.

Lavender Gourami / *Trichogaster sp.*

This is a very new colour variety of the Gold gourami. Commercial breeders in the Far East found a few of these in their broods, separated them and then worked on them until they bred true. With the pink to lilac colouration on the main parts of their body, and orange on the lower parts, they make a very bright addition to your aquarium. They are typical bubble-nest breeders but do not produce as many eggs as the other standard gouramies. Like most other gouramies they are quite hardy and very easy to keep.

Feeding

They will take all types of food, but thrive on a wide variety of flakes, frozen and live foods. Ensure that vegetable foods are part of their diet. Live foods such as bloodworm, daphnia, glassworm and tubifex are very good for these fish.

ORIGIN
asia

TEMPERATURE RANGE
71.5–79°F (22–26°C)

COMMUNITY
very good

ADULT SIZE
female 3 $\frac{1}{2}$ in (9cm)
male 3 $\frac{3}{4}$ in (9.5cm)

DIET
all foods

EASE OF KEEPING
9/10

PH RANGE
6.8–7.5

Moonlight Gourami / *Trichogaster microlepis*

ORIGIN
asia

TEMPERATURE RANGE
68–79°F (20–26°C)

COMMUNITY
very good

ADULT SIZE
female 4 ³/₄ in (12cm)
male 6 in (15cm)

DIET
all foods

EASE OF KEEPING
9/10

PH RANGE
6.8–7.5

The upper body of this fish has an olive green colouration and the lower half is totally silver. As they grow into adults, this colour intensifies until the silver is very mirror-like. The snout becomes extended as the fish grows, to the point of looking deformed. However, this is the snout's natural shape. This usually only applies to the male. The female has rounded fins and is thicker in the body.

Feeding
They will take all types of food, but thrive on a wide variety of flakes, frozen and live foods. Ensure that vegetable foods are part of their diet. Live foods such as bloodworm, daphnia, glassworm and tubifex are very good for these fish.

Snakeskin Gourami / *Trichogaster pectoralis*

This fish is quite widespread throughout Asia, including Thailand, Cambodia and Malaysia. As with most of the gouramies, they can exist in polluted rivers and streams because they breathe air from the surface but that does not mean that this is good for them. When these fish breed, normally there is quite a lot of parental care. The adults both maintain the bubble-nest, constantly rebuilding it, and as the fry drop out of the nest, they will pick them up in their mouth and spit them back into the nest.

Feeding

They will take all types of food, but thrive on a wide variety of flakes, frozen and live foods. Ensure that vegetable foods are part of their diet. Live foods such as bloodworm, daphnia, glassworm and tubifex are very good for these fish.

ORIGIN
asia

TEMPERATURE RANGE
68–79°F (20–26°C)

COMMUNITY
very good

ADULT SIZE
female 7 in (18cm)
male 7 in (18cm)

DIET
all foods

EASE OF KEEPING
9/10

PH RANGE
6.8–7.5

CICHLIDS

Albino Kribensis / *Pelmatochromis kribensis*

ORIGIN
africa

TEMPERATURE RANGE
70–79°F (21–26°C)

COMMUNITY
good

ADULT SIZE
female 3 in (8cm)
male 4 in (10cm)

DIET
all foods

EASE OF KEEPING
9/10

PH RANGE
6.8–7.5

The Kribensis, like most cichlids, are very hardy fish. They can be territorial and will certainly be so if they decide to pair up and breed. They like to have places to hide, such as a cave. This is where they will also lay their eggs. They take great care of the eggs and the fry once the eggs have hatched. Any other fish coming close will be chased away in no uncertain terms. When the fry get to about 10-14 days old, the adults will start to let them go. The youngsters are very easy to care for and grow on.

Male

Feeding

They will take all types of food, but thrive on a wide variety of flakes, frozen and live foods. Live foods such as bloodworm, daphnia, glassworm and tubifex are very good for these fish.

Female

CICHLIDS

Freiberg's Peacock Cichlid / *Aulonocara jacobfreibergi*

ORIGIN
lake malawi (africa)

TEMPERATURE RANGE
71.5–79°F (22–26°C)

COMMUNITY
good in species tank only

ADULT SIZE
female 4 ³/₄ in (12cm)
male 6 in (15cm)

DIET
all foods

EASE OF KEEPING
8/10

PH RANGE
6.8–7.5

As with most of the Lake Malawi cichlids, these are cave dwellers. The aquarium needs to be set up to include large stones and rocks so that there are plenty of caves for these fish to select as their own areas. They can all be extremely territorial, although not always. Most of the cichlids from Malawi are quite vividly patterned in the adult stage to put off predators. The females are generally quite bland in appearance compared to the males and it is best to keep them in pairs.

Feeding

They will take all types of food, but thrive on a wide variety of flakes, frozen and live foods. Live foods such as bloodworm, daphnia, glassworm and tubifex are very good for these fish.

Blue Acara Cichlid / *Aequidens pulcher*

This fish has been known for many years. Although it really needs to be kept with fish larger than itself, if you keep it very well fed on solid meaty foods, you may well be able to keep it with other fish, such as swordtails – but certainly nothing smaller. If you see any problems, then transfer it to another aquarium immediately. If they do not like the way you have set the gravel up in the aquarium, then they will move it around themselves until they are happy with it.

Feeding

They will take all types of food, but thrive on a wide variety of flakes, frozen and live foods. Live foods such as bloodworm, daphnia, glassworm and tubifex are very good for these fish. Small earthworms are also a favourite.

ORIGIN
south america

TEMPERATURE RANGE
71.5–79°F (22–26°C)

COMMUNITY
only with larger fish

ADULT SIZE
female 4 ³/₄ in (12cm)
male 6 in (15cm)

DIET
all foods

EASE OF KEEPING
9/10

PH RANGE
6.8–7.5

CICHLIDS

Blue Diamond Discus / *Symphysodon sp.*

ORIGIN
south america

TEMPERATURE RANGE
75–80.5°F (24–27°C)

COMMUNITY
very good

ADULT SIZE
female 6 in (15cm)
male 6 in (15cm)

DIET
all foods

EASE OF KEEPING
8/10

PH RANGE
6.8–7.0

This is just one of many colour variations of this fish. Colours range from green to reds to pinks and recently whites. They prefer slightly softer water but can, over a period of time, have small water changes until they become accustomed to tap water. There are stories of this fish being very difficult to keep, but if the water conditions are good and if they are fed high quality food then you should not have problems with them. If you keep them with a shoal of Cardinal tetras or Emperor tetras, they will complement each other.

Feeding
They will take all types of food, but thrive on a wide variety of flakes, frozen and live foods. Live foods such as bloodworm, daphnia, glassworm and tubifex are excellent.

Snakeskin Discus / *Symphysodon sp.*

There are now many high quality hybrid forms of discus being bred, mainly in the Far East. When breeding these fish, do not use two different colours because their parentage will be unknown to you and you will not know what you will produce. Discus will need to be in an aquarium without other fish to spawn and this they normally do on a terracotta pot. When the eggs hatch out, the fry feed from mucus created by the adults on the sides of their bodies. They will normally feed on this for up to 14 days, at which time very fine food such as newly hatched brine shrimp have to be fed to them.

Feeding

They will take all types of food, but thrive on a wide variety of flakes, frozen and live foods. Live foods such as bloodworm, daphnia, glassworm and tubifex are very good for these fish.

ORIGIN
south america

TEMPERATURE RANGE
75–80.5°F (24–27°C)

COMMUNITY
very good

ADULT SIZE
female 6 in (15cm)
male 6 in (15cm)

DIET
all foods

EASE OF KEEPING
8/10

PH RANGE
6.8–7.0

CICHLIDS

Temporale Cichlid / *Cichlasoma temporale*

ORIGIN
south america

TEMPERATURE RANGE
75–80.5°F (24–27°F)

COMMUNITY
very good with larger
fish

ADULT SIZE
female 12 in (30cm)
male 12 in (30cm)

DIET
all foods

EASE OF KEEPING
9/10

PH RANGE
6.8–7.2

To keep this fish, an aquarium of at least 48 in (122cm) long and 18 in (46cm) deep is required. Although they grow to quite a large size, these fish are very docile towards other fish, except when breeding. The only true way to sex them is when the male becomes fully adult. He will then grow a lump on his head, known as a 'cranial hump'. The female does not get this. Bright red blotches around the front and lower front of the body is the usual colouration as they become adults. The photograph shows a juvenile.

Feeding

They will take all types of food, but thrive on a wide variety of flakes, frozen and live foods. Live foods such as bloodworm, daphnia, glassworm and tubifex are very good for these fish. They will also accept small quantities of grated beef heart.

Chequerboard Cichlid / *Crenicara filamentosa*

Although this variety can be very hard to find, when they are available it is best to buy one male and several females. Good quality water conditions are required to keep this fish at its best. The male grows to be the larger fish and his tail is forked with extensions to both lobes of the tail. His fins also have red patterning in them, whereas the fins of the female are transparent. The stock of this fish that you will see available is almost certainly going to be wild import.

Feeding

They will take all types of food, but thrive on a wide variety of flakes, frozen and live foods. Live foods such as bloodworm, daphnia, glassworm, brine shrimp and tubifex are excellent.

ORIGIN
south america

TEMPERATURE RANGE
72–80.5°F (23–27°C)

COMMUNITY
very good

ADULT SIZE
female 2 ³/₄ in (7cm)
male 3 ¹/₂ in (9cm)

DIET
all foods

EASE OF KEEPING
8/10

PH RANGE
6.8–7.0

CICHLIDS

Geophagus argyrostictus / *Geophagus argyrostictus*

ORIGIN
south america

TEMPERATURE RANGE
75–80.5°F (24–27°C)

COMMUNITY
very good

ADULT SIZE
female 6 in (15cm)
male 6 in (15cm)

DIET
all foods

EASE OF KEEPING
8/10

PH RANGE
6.8–7.0

The Geophagus group of fish is commonly called 'Eartheaters'. They have a habit of picking up mouthfuls of the substrate and moving it to other areas of the aquarium. They also sift through it, tasting for food. Do not put rocks or stones on top of each other in the aquarium, as they will inevitably fall over and could damage the tank. They are a very graceful fish, moving around the aquarium quite serenely. Fish larger than platies are normally fine to mix with them.

Feeding
They will take all types of food, but thrive on a wide variety of flakes, frozen and live foods. Live foods such as bloodworm, daphnia, glassworm and tubifex are very good for these fish.

Geophagus / *Geophagus sp.*

Sexing these fish is quite difficult because generally the only way to see the difference is by the length of the dorsal and anal fin. The extensions on these fins will only start to become apparent as they grow from juvenile to semi-adult and, because they are a slow growing fish, that can be quite a wait, although it is well-worth it. Keep four or five together as a group and they will do well.

Feeding
They will take all types of food, but thrive on a wide variety of flakes, frozen and live foods. Live foods such as bloodworm, daphnia, glassworm and tubifex are very good for these fish.

ORIGIN
south america

TEMPERATURE RANGE
75–80.5°F (24–27°C)

COMMUNITY
very good

ADULT SIZE
female 6 in (15cm)
male 6 in (15cm)

DIET
all foods

EASE OF KEEPING
8/10

PH RANGE
6.8–7.0

Obliquidens Zebra / *Astatotilapia latifasciata*

ORIGIN
lake kyogo (africa)

TEMPERATURE RANGE
75–80.5°F (24–27°C)

COMMUNITY
good with other
african cichlids

ADULT SIZE
female 4 ³/₄ in (12cm)
male 4 ³/₄ in (12cm)

DIET
all foods

EASE OF KEEPING
8/10

PH RANGE
7.5–8.0

Generally, all of the lake cichlids from Africa require a much higher pH than normal community fish. The pH can be as high as 9.0 in some of the lakes and you must remember that most of the South American fish that are available cannot live in water with a pH level that high. If you wish to keep this type of fish, it is very easy to maintain the pH to that level by placing tuffa rock in your aquarium. An aquarium set up specifically for African cichlids looks really attractive with all of the different colours on this type of fish.

Feeding

They will take all types of food, but thrive on a wide variety of flakes, frozen and live foods. Live foods such as bloodworm, daphnia, glassworm and tubifex are very good for these fish.

Jewel Cichlid / *Hemichromis bimaculatus*

The common name of Jewel cichlid is very deservedly given because of the colouration of this fish. Its bright red body is covered with reflective spotting and it is stunning to see. Unfortunately, it has a bad reputation for being aggressive to anything smaller than itself. With larger fish in the aquarium that stand up for themselves, it is a totally different fish and will leave everything alone. They will breed quite readily and will lay 300–400 eggs. Very hardy fish.

ORIGIN
liberia (africa)

TEMPERATURE RANGE
73–80.5°F (23–27°C)

COMMUNITY
only with larger fish

ADULT SIZE
female 6 in (15cm)
male 6 in (15cm)

DIET
all foods

EASE OF KEEPING
9/10

PH RANGE
6.8–7.5

Feeding

They will take all types of food, but thrive on a wide variety of flakes, frozen and live foods. Live foods such as bloodworm, daphnia, glassworm and tubifex are excellent.

Frontosa / *Cyphotilapia frontosa*

This is a very interesting fish in that in its habitat of Lake Tanganyika, the adults are found at depths as far down as 195 ft (60m). When these fish are captured in the wild, they have to go through decompression, which can take up to three days. It is thought that, when young, the fish stays in the shallower waters of the lake but as it gets older, it progressively goes deeper. They are very lethargic fish, only using energy if they have to, which makes them seem very graceful in the aquarium. A very large aquarium is required if you are to keep them.

Feeding

They will take all types of food, but thrive on a wide variety of flakes, frozen and live foods. Live foods such as bloodworm, daphnia, glassworm and tubifex are very good for these fish.

ORIGIN
lake tanganyika (africa)

TEMPERATURE RANGE
73–79°F (23–26°C)

COMMUNITY
good with larger fish

ADULT SIZE
female 13 ¹/₂ in (35cm)
male 13 ¹/₂ in (35cm)

DIET
all foods

EASE OF KEEPING
8/10

PH RANGE
6.8–7.5

Dickfelds Julie / *Julidochromis dickfeldi*

ORIGIN
lake tanganyika (africa)

TEMPERATURE RANGE
73–79°F (23–26°C)

COMMUNITY
very good

ADULT SIZE
female 3 in (8cm)
male 3 $\frac{1}{2}$ in (9cm)

DIET
all foods

EASE OF KEEPING
9/10

PH RANGE
6.8–7.5

The Julidochromis group of fish are all very pretty. They also do not need the water to have high pH levels. They are quite happy to be in a community aquarium as long as they have places to hide away. Plenty of plants and caves are ideal for them. They will spawn in caves and defend that area quite vigorously.

Feeding

They will take all types of food, but thrive on a wide variety of flakes, frozen and live foods. Live foods such as bloodworm, daphnia, glassworm and tubifex are very good for these fish.

Marliers Julie / *Julidochromis marlieri*

The male of this species develops a nuchal hump on its head as it becomes adult. This is just like a bump on the back of the head. It is natural so do not worry that something is wrong. The female does not get this. These fish will spawn but only when they are ready. They do not lay many eggs, normally around 80-100. Small terracotta flower pots are the ideal thing for them to spawn in

Feeding

They will take all types of food, but thrive on a wide variety of flakes, frozen and live foods. Live foods such as bloodworm, daphnia, glassworm and tubifex are very good for these fish.

ORIGIN
lake tanganyika (africa)

TEMPERATURE RANGE
73–79°F (23–26°C)

COMMUNITY
very good

ADULT SIZE
female 4 ³/₄ in (12cm)
male 5 in (13cm)

DIET
all foods

EASE OF KEEPING
9/10

PH RANGE
6.8–7.5

CICHLIDS

Striped or Four striped Julie / *Julidochromis regani*

ORIGIN
lake tanganyika (africa)

TEMPERATURE RANGE
73–79°F (23–26°C)

COMMUNITY
very good

ADULT SIZE
female 4 ³/₄ in (12cm)
male 5 in (13cm)

DIET
all foods

EASE OF KEEPING
19/10

PH RANGE
6.8–7.5

As with some of the other fish in the Julidochromis group, this fish also has some varieties where the pattern or colour changes slightly, depending on where it originates. This sometimes makes identification difficult. If you keep them with other fish they will do well, but if you keep them in a specific species tank they will hide away nearly all the time and you will not see the beauty of them. Feeding them free swimming food such as daphnia or glassworm will certainly make them very active.

Feeding

They will take all types of food, but thrive on a wide variety of flakes, frozen and live foods. Live foods such as bloodworm, daphnia, glassworm and tubifex are excellent.

Yellow Labido / *Labidochromis coeruleus "Yellow"*

This fish is quite at home in an aquarium set up with rocks and stones forming many caves and hideaways for it to explore, or an aquarium set up with a sand substrate and a bed of giant straight vallis. There are a number of colour forms of this fish, depending on which part of Lake Malawi it comes from. Many of them are quite simply named after that very small area. This yellow form is the most common.

Feeding

They will take all types of food, but thrive on a wide variety of flakes, frozen and live foods. Live foods such as bloodworm, daphnia, glassworm and tubifex are very good for these fish.

ORIGIN
lake malawi (africa)

TEMPERATURE RANGE
73–80.5°F (23–27°C)

COMMUNITY
good in african species tank

ADULT SIZE
female 3 1/4 in (8cm)
male 4 in (10cm)

DIET
all foods

EASE OF KEEPING
9/10

PH RANGE
6.8–7.5

Acei Yellow / *Pseudotropheus acei "Yellow"*

ORIGIN
lake malawi (africa)

TEMPERATURE RANGE
73–80.5°F (23–27°C)

COMMUNITY
good in african species tank

ADULT SIZE
female 3 ¹/₂ in (9cm)
male 4 in (10cm)

DIET
all foods

EASE OF KEEPING
9/10

PH RANGE
6.8–7.5

Again, this fish is quite at home in an aquarium set up with rocks and stones forming many caves and hideaways for it to explore, or an aquarium set up with a sand substrate and a bed of giant straight vallis. When breeding in the aquarium, it has been noted that the male digs a pit in the sand substrate between large stones or rocks and the pair will spawn there, but in the wild it has not been seen to do this.

Feeding
They will take all types of food, but thrive on a wide variety of flakes, frozen and live foods. Live foods such as bloodworm, daphnia, glassworm and tubifex are very good for these fish.

Elongatus / *Pseudotropheus elongatus "Neon Spot"*

This fish is very easy to keep and maintain. It needs lots of rocks, caves and crevices to explore and settle into. It is quite widespread in its natural habitat with many different location forms. These are mainly slight changes in the colour or patterns on the body. Most of these fish have a deep blue body colour with black bars running top to bottom of the body. There are two varieties that have a yellow base colour, again with black bars.

Feeding

They will take all types of food, but thrive on a wide variety of flakes, frozen and live foods. Live foods such as bloodworm, daphnia, glassworm and tubifex are very good for these fish.

ORIGIN
lake malawi (africa)

TEMPERATURE RANGE
73–80.5°F (23–27°C)

COMMUNITY
good in african species
tank

ADULT SIZE
female 4 ³/₄ in (12cm)
male 5 in (13cm)

DIET
all foods

EASE OF KEEPING
9/10

PH RANGE
6.8–7.5

CICHLIDS

Eduard's Mbuna / *Pseudotropheus socolofi*

ORIGIN
lake malawi (africa)

TEMPERATURE RANGE
73–80.5°F (23–27°C)

COMMUNITY
good in african species tank

ADULT SIZE
female 5 ¼ in (13cm)
male 6 in (15cm)

DIET
all foods

EASE OF KEEPING
9/10

PH RANGE
6.8–7.5

Again, this fish is very easy to keep and maintain. In its natural habitat it comes from the crossover area between a sand substrate and a rock base. You have to be careful with this fish in your aquarium because it has a habit of digging caves out of the sand substrate beneath any rock that you have in your tank. This can be very dangerous if the rocks fall and they may also damage the aquarium. It is a good idea, when building the interior of your aquarium, to bond the rocks and stones together using aquarium sealant.

Feeding

They will take all types of food, but thrive on a wide variety of flakes, frozen and live foods. Live foods such as bloodworm, daphnia, glassworm and tubifex are very good for these fish.

White Spotted Cichlid / *Tropheus duboisi*

When these fish are juveniles the pattern on the body is spotted; as they become adults the body becomes one solid colour, with a single wide bar in the centre of the body from top to bottom. As you can see from the photographs, when this fish is first moved it changes colour to what is generally known as a fright pattern. The pictures shown are of the same fish. Within about 10 minutes of being moved, the colour changed back. This is not uncommon with many African cichlids.

ORIGIN
lake tanganyika (africa)

TEMPERATURE RANGE
73–80.5°F (23–27°C)

COMMUNITY
good in african species tank

ADULT SIZE
female 4 ³/₄ in (12cm)
male 5 in (13cm)

DIET
all foods

EASE OF KEEPING
8/10

PH RANGE
6.8–7.5

Fright pattern

Juvenile

Feeding

They will take all types of food, but thrive on a
wide variety of flakes, frozen and live foods. Live
foods such as bloodworm, daphnia, glassworm
and tubifex are very good for these fish.

Ruby Cichlid / *Microgeophagus peruviensis*

This fish, to my knowledge, has only been available in the hobby for the past couple of years. It is very similar to the Bolivian ram (*M. altispinosa*). This one does not have the dark spot in the middle of the body. The body is much lighter in colour with a yellowy area under the chin through to the belly area. I have found it to be a timid fish when first introduced to the aquarium and it takes quite a time to settle down and find its place. Once settled, it is very peaceful. They do better in a small shoal.

Feeding

They will take all types of food, but thrive on a wide variety of flakes, frozen and live foods. Live foods such as bloodworm, daphnia, glassworm and tubifex are very good for these fish.

ORIGIN
south america

TEMPERATURE RANGE
71.5–80.5°F (22–27°C)

COMMUNITY
very good

ADULT SIZE
female 2 $^3/_4$ in (7cm)
male 3 $^1/_2$ in (9cm)

DIET
all foods

EASE OF KEEPING
8/10

PH RANGE
6.8–7.5

Triangle Cichlid / *Uaru amphiacanthoides*

ORIGIN
south america

TEMPERATURE RANGE
73–80.5°F (23–27°C)

COMMUNITY
very good with larger fish

ADULT SIZE
female 12 in (30cm)
male 12 in (30cm)

DIET
all foods

EASE OF KEEPING
8/10

PH RANGE
6.8–7.5

Purely because of the potential size of this fish, it is much better to keep it solely with larger fish. You will need an aquarium at least 48 in (122cm) long so that the growth of this fish is not stunted. When they spawn, they do so on a large plant leaf or piece of slate. When the fry hatch, as with the discus fish, they will feed from secretions on the body of the parents. When they are young, the body colour is a mottled pattern. As they become adult the colour changes so that the upper body is olive-grey with a large brown triangular patch on the lower half of the body.

Feeding
They will take all types of food, but thrive on a wide variety of flakes, frozen and live foods. Live foods such as bloodworm, daphnia, glassworm and tubifex are very good for these fish.

Festivum or Festive Cichlid / *Mesanauta festivus*

This fish, for some unknown reason, has seemed to be a 'fashion fish' over the years. I have always found it to be popular and very easy to keep and maintain. Two or three together in an aquarium is probably the best way to keep them. They will co-exist quite happily with fish such as Cardinal tetras and rummynose. They are egg layers and will lay on small rocks or stones. They will then care for the eggs by fanning them and picking out any that have fungus on them. When the fry hatch out, they will usher them into a corner of the aquarium and keep them there until they are too big to do so.

Feeding

They will take all types of food, but thrive on a wide variety of flakes, frozen and live foods. Live foods such as bloodworm, daphnia, glassworm and tubifex are very good for these fish.

ORIGIN
south america

TEMPERATURE RANGE
73–79°F (23–26°C)

COMMUNITY
very good

ADULT SIZE
female 5 ³/₄ in (15cm)
male 5 ³/₄ in (15cm)

DIET
all foods

EASE OF KEEPING
8/10

PH RANGE
6.8–7.5

CICHLIDS

Angel Fish / *Pterophyllum scalare*

ORIGIN
south america

TEMPERATURE RANGE
71.5–79°F (22–26°C)

COMMUNITY
very good when small

ADULT SIZE
female 3 ³/₄ in (9.5cm)
male 3 ³/₄ in (9.5cm)

DIET
all foods

EASE OF KEEPING
9/10

PH RANGE
6.8–7.5

With the amount of commercial breeding that goes on with these fish, it would seem that some of their aggressive traits have been bred out. If they are fed very regularly with high quality foods, I have noted that they tend to leave the smaller fish alone and have the odd squabble amongst themselves without actually do any damage to each other. They are normally available in an aquarium shop from about 1–1¹/₂ in (3–4cm) upwards. If maintained and fed correctly, the growth rate is quite good.

When a male and female decide to pair off they will pick an area that they will spawn on. Using their mouths, they will scrupulously clean that area and, at the same time, defend it from the other fish in the aquarium quite voraciously. Be wary of this action, as it does not always mean that it is a proper pairing. Two females will do these actions together, leading you to think that you have a true pair. Immature pairs will often spawn

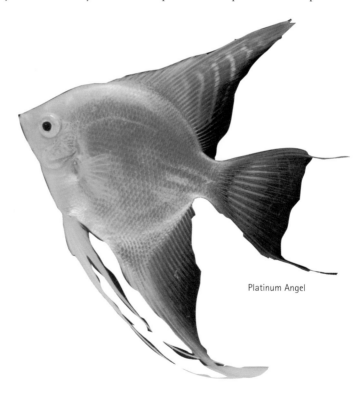

Platinum Angel

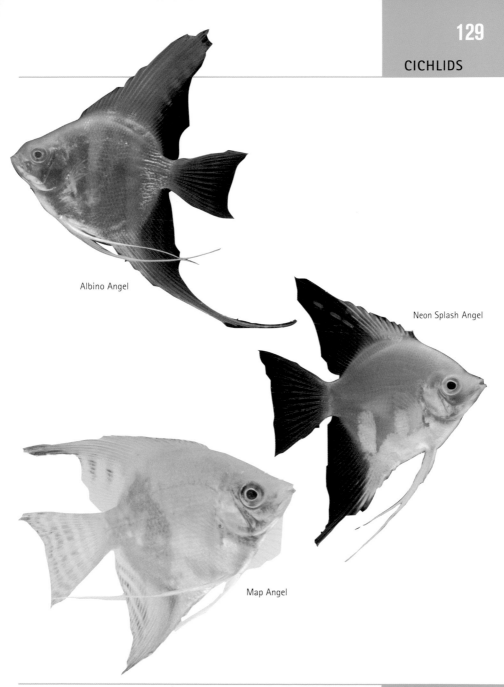

Albino Angel

Neon Splash Angel

Map Angel

together but then within a very short period of time will eat the eggs. If you find this to be the case with a particular pair, next time they spawn remove the eggs into a smaller aquarium and hopefully the eggs will hatch there. You will have to treat that aquarium for any fungal infection as normally the adults would pick off and eat any eggs that are infected. You must also ensure that there is a vigorous air supply around the eggs.

They will lay anything up to 300 eggs. If you are lucky enough to hatch the eggs you must be ready with enough of the correct type of food. They will need infusoria for the first 5–6 days and then slightly larger food, such as newly hatched brine shrimp. Your local dealer should be able to supply these foods. After about another week, you should be able to get them onto crushed flake foods. At about 7–8 weeks old, the young should be big enough for your local dealer to be interested in buying them from you.

Feeding

They will take all types of food, but thrive on a wide variety of flakes, frozen and live foods. Live foods such as bloodworm, daphnia, glassworm and tubifex are very good for these fish.

Leopard Angel

Black Angel

Giant Brochis / *Brochis britskii*

This is one of the largest fish in this group, growing to around 3 ¾ in (9.5cm). They tend to be a little more expensive than the other fish in the group and for that reason we do not see them very often. They are very seasonal in their availability because they are imported from the wild. The only difference between male and female can be seen by looking at the fish from above, when you will see that the male is the slimmer of the two. It is believed that when they spawn, they will lay the eggs on any solid object, including the glass of the aquarium, and there is absolutely no parental care.

Feeding

They will take all types of food, but thrive on a wide variety of flakes, frozen and live foods. Live foods such as bloodworm, daphnia, glassworm and tubifex are very good for these fish. Catfish pellets and tablets are also excellent.

ORIGIN
south america

TEMPERATURE RANGE
70–77°F (21–25°C)

COMMUNITY
excellent

ADULT SIZE
female 3 ³/₄ in (9.5cm)
male 3 ³/₄ in (9.5cm)

DIET
all foods

EASE OF KEEPING
9/10

PH RANGE
6.8–7.5

Hog-nosed Brochis / *Brochis multiradiatus*

ORIGIN
south america

TEMPERATURE RANGE
70–77°F (21–25°C)

COMMUNITY
excellent

ADULT SIZE
female 3 ³/₄ in (9.5cm)
male 3 ³/₄ in (9.5cm)

DIET
all foods

EASE OF KEEPING
9/10

PH RANGE
6.8–7.5

This is very similar to *B. britskii* except that the dorsal fin has more rays and the nose is much longer. Again, it is a very solid fish and the sexual differences are the same as *B. britskii*. The barbels are very long for this type of fish but they use them to great effect going through the substrate for small titbits of food. Food such as bloodworm and tubifex are ideal for conditioning this fish for breeding. There are not many reports concerning the spawning of this fish but it is believed again to be the same as *B. britskii*.

Feeding

They will take all types of food, but thrive on a wide variety of flakes, frozen and live foods. Live foods such as bloodworm, daphnia, glassworm and tubifex are very good for these fish. Catfish pellets and tablets are also excellent.

Acrensis Corydoras / *Corydoras acrensis*

There are no known aggressive fish within the corydoras group. So it is quite safe to keep as many different species together as your aquarium will allow, subject to sufficient filtration, aeration, feeding and maintenance. Where most of the corydoras are concerned, it is very easy to tell the difference between male and female. The female is much rounder in the belly area when well fed and conditioned. Because of the diversity of patterns within this group, I find them extremely interesting to study. If you wanted to keep just one kind of fish with a lot of variety, then this is the group for you.

Feeding

They will take all types of food, but thrive on a wide variety of flakes, frozen and live foods. Live foods such as bloodworm, daphnia, glassworm and tubifex are very good for these fish. Catfish pellets and tablets are also excellent.

ORIGIN
south america

TEMPERATURE RANGE
70–79°F (21–26°C)

COMMUNITY
excellent

ADULT SIZE
female 3 in (8cm)
male 3 in (8cm)

DIET
all foods

EASE OF KEEPING
9/10

PH RANGE
6.8–7.5

Adolfos Corydoras / *Corydoras adolfoi*

ORIGIN
south america

TEMPERATURE RANGE
70–79°F (21–26°C)

COMMUNITY
excellent

ADULT SIZE
female 2 $^3/_4$ in (7cm)
male 2 $^3/_4$ in (7cm)

DIET
all foods

EASE OF KEEPING
9/10

PH RANGE
6.8–7.5

This is a particularly nice fish with its contrasting beigish cream body, black bar running across the back and bar through the eye. There is also a gold blotch between the bar through the eye and the dorsal fin. Looking at the fish from above you will see which one is the female very easily. Do not keep this type of fish on a spa gravel substrate as the barbels will wear away and will not re-grow. This fish is normally only available for about four months of the year from the wild, which is usually about six weeks after the end of the rainy season.

Feeding

They will take all types of food, but thrive on a wide variety of flakes, frozen and live foods. Live foods such as bloodworm, daphnia, glassworm and tubifex are very good for these fish. Catfish pellets and tablets are also excellent.

Ashers Corydoras / *Corydoras "asher" reynoldsi*

This fish was originally found by an exporter in Manaus, Brazil. They have been rare for quite a long time but have recently been easier to buy. As with all of the corydoras, they do much better if the substrate is silica sand. This is light enough for them to move around and forage in for food. Sand is also the natural substrate for them in the wild. They have a very snub nose with three pairs of quite long barbels.

Feeding

They will take all types of food, but thrive on a wide variety of flakes, frozen and live foods. Live foods such as bloodworm, daphnia, glassworm and tubifex are very good for these fish. Catfish pellets and tablets are also excellent.

ORIGIN
south america

TEMPERATURE RANGE
70–79°F (21–26°C)

COMMUNITY
excellent

ADULT SIZE
female 2 ³/₄ in (7cm)
male 2 ³/₄ in (7cm)

DIET
all foods

EASE OF KEEPING
9/10

PH RANGE
6.8–7.5

Banded Corydoras / *Corydoras barbatus*

ORIGIN
south america

TEMPERATURE RANGE
70–79°F (21–26°C)

COMMUNITY
excellent

ADULT SIZE
female 4 ³/₄ in (12cm)
male 4 ³/₄ in (12cm)

DIET
all foods

EASE OF KEEPING
9/10

PH RANGE
6.8–7.5

This is a very long and slender corydoras, which is quite different from the others of this group. There are a couple of location varieties, which are available from time to time – the Gold Line barbatus and the Black Line barbatus. This fish is known to breed quite regularly. The female swims up the glass and lays sticky eggs and the male then follows and fertilises them. When the eggs hatch, the fry are quite easy to feed and grow on.

Feeding

They will take all types of food, but thrive on a wide variety of flakes, frozen and live foods. Live foods such as bloodworm, daphnia, glassworm and tubifex are very good for these fish. Catfish pellets and tablets are also excellent.

CORYDORAS

Blochs Corydoras / *Corydoras blochi vittatus*

ORIGIN
south america

TEMPERATURE RANGE
70–79°F (21–26°C)

COMMUNITY
excellent

ADULT SIZE
female 2 1/4 in (6cm)
male 2 1/4 in (6cm)

DIET
all foods

EASE OF KEEPING
9/10

PH RANGE
6.8–7.5

This is another fish that is only seen on a seasonal basis. They are normally available for about eight weeks twice a year, both occasions being just after the rainy seasons finish. You will have to check with your local aquatic dealer when this is, because it changes from year to year. The great majority of the corydoras that you will see in your local dealer's aquariums are imported, as there is relatively little commercial breeding done with these fish. Breeding of corydoras is quite a challenge but can be done.

Feeding

They will take all types of food, but thrive on a wide variety of flakes, frozen and live foods. Live foods such as bloodworm, daphnia, glassworm and tubifex are very good for these fish. Catfish pellets and tablets are also excellent.

Burgess Corydoras / *Corydoras burgessi*

This is very close in colouration and markings to *C. adolphoi*. The only noticeable difference is the lack of the black band across its back and the shorter snout. This is quite a new fish to the hobby and it is often identified incorrectly. The fish are usually imported in amongst other fish that look very similar and then have to be sorted and picked out. A small shoal of four or five of them will look very attractive in your aquarium. If you decide to keep them on a gravel substrate, you should use pea gravel so the fish does not damage their barbels as they forage across it looking for food.

Feeding

They will take all types of food, but thrive on a wide variety of flakes, frozen and live foods. Live foods such as bloodworm, daphnia, glassworm and tubifex are very good for these fish. Catfish pellets and tablets are also excellent.

ORIGIN
south america

TEMPERATURE RANGE
70–79°F (21–26°C)

COMMUNITY
excellent

ADULT SIZE
female 2 ³/₄ in (7cm)
male 2 ³/₄ in (7cm)

DIET
all foods

EASE OF KEEPING
9/10

PH RANGE
6.8–7.5

Tail Spot Corydoras / *Corydoras caudimaculatus*

ORIGIN
south america

TEMPERATURE RANGE
70–79°F (21–26°C)

COMMUNITY
excellent

ADULT SIZE
female 2 ³/₄ in (7cm)
male 2 ³/₄ in (7cm)

DIET
all foods

EASE OF KEEPING
9/10

PH RANGE
6.8–7.5

This is one of the smaller corydoras, only growing to about 2 ¾ in (7cm). When they are juveniles, the spots are quite large. As the fish grows the spots seem to break up and become quite fine. Not all fish are named after people or places but instead are given a Latin species name that is a full or partial description of that fish. In this case, the species name is *caudimaculatus*. *Caudi* means the tail area and *maculatus* means spot or blotch. This is how it got its common name of Tail Spot corydoras.

Feeding

They will take all types of food, but thrive on a wide variety of flakes, frozen and live foods. Live foods such as bloodworm, daphnia, glassworm and tubifex are very good for these fish. Catfish pellets and tablets are also excellent.

Delphax Corydoras / *Corydoras delphax*

There are about seven or eight location varieties of this fish but they are all predominantly the same pattern. However, differences occur in the density of the coloured spots on the fish. When you have two or three different types together this is very noticeable. As the fish gets older, the dorsal fin becomes elongated. It starts to extend as the fish goes from semi-adult to full adult. The bigger the fish gets, the bigger the first ray of the dorsal fin. When catching this group of fish, always be careful not to stab yourself with the dorsal or pectoral fins as they are like needles and can be quite painful for a few seconds.

Feeding

They will take all types of food, but thrive on a wide variety of flakes, frozen and live foods. Live foods such as bloodworm, daphnia, glassworm and tubifex are very good for these fish. Catfish pellets and tablets are also excellent.

ORIGIN
south america

TEMPERATURE RANGE
70–79°F (21–26°C)

COMMUNITY
excellent

ADULT SIZE
female 2 $^3/_4$ in (7cm)
male 2 $^3/_4$ in (7cm)

DIET
all foods

EASE OF KEEPING
9/10

PH RANGE
6.8–7.5

Gosses Corydoras / *Corydoras gossei*

ORIGIN
south america

TEMPERATURE RANGE
70–79°F (21–26°C)

COMMUNITY
excellent

ADULT SIZE
female 3 in (8cm)
male 3 in (8cm)

DIET
all foods

EASE OF KEEPING
9/10

PH RANGE
6.8–7.5

The females of this species, when looked at from above, are extremely wide in the body just behind the head. When in top condition the first rays of the dorsal fin and the pectoral fins are bright orange, which really shows off the darker plain body colour. They can be a problem to transport if more than one is in a bag. Always ask your supplier to pack them in a larger than usual sized bag, and to pack them individually. Because of the shock and stress factor, they are known to give off a chemical into the water, which triggers the other fish to do the same. This will make them die if they are not put into your aquarium very quickly. If packed properly, they are not a problem and are well-worth buying.

Feeding
They will take all types of food, but thrive on a wide variety of flakes, frozen and live foods. Live foods such as bloodworm, daphnia, glassworm and tubifex are very good for these fish. Catfish pellets and tablets are also excellent

Pretty Corydoras / *Corydoras gracilis*

This fish has been known for a very long time, but until recently was thought to be extinct in the wild. Very recently, I received a shipment of this fish which had been offered to me under another species name. This turned out to be a local name in Brazil. After further investigation, it would seem that the populations of this fish move from area to area, which makes them difficult to catch. They will settle in one place, breed, and the youngsters will grow and then they move again Normally, corydoras stay within a defined area of a stream or river, but this seems not to be the case with this fish. They are an exceptionally pretty fish, with a very attractive gold line running the length of the body just below the crown of the back.

Feeding

They will take all types of food, but thrive on a wide variety of flakes, frozen and live foods. Live foods such as bloodworm, daphnia, glassworm and tubifex are very good for these fish. Catfish pellets and tablets are also excellent.

ORIGIN
south america

TEMPERATURE RANGE
70–79°F (21–26°C)

COMMUNITY
excellent

ADULT SIZE
female 1 ¹/₂ in (4cm)
male 1 ¹/₂ in (4cm)

DIET
all foods

EASE OF KEEPING
9/10

PH RANGE
6.8–7.5

Leopard Corydoras / *Corydoras leopardus*

ORIGIN
south america

TEMPERATURE RANGE
70–79°F (21–26°C)

COMMUNITY
excellent

ADULT SIZE
female 3 in (8cm)
male 3 in (8cm)

DIET
all foods

EASE OF KEEPING
9/10

PH RANGE
6.8–7.5

Whoever discovered this fish originally saw in their mind a leopard, purely because of the spots, and that is how this fish got its name. When in good condition, the belly area is a creamy white and the body has many spots. These are jet black with a large blotch on the upper part of the dorsal fin, which is also jet black. The spots can join together to create a semi-reticulated pattern. These fish look exceptionally good if there is a large shoal of them. They are also quite hardy and, as with many other corydoras, they are ideal to go into a newly set-up aquarium.

Feeding

They will take all types of food, but thrive on a wide variety of flakes, frozen and live foods. Live foods such as bloodworm, daphnia, glassworm and tubifex are very good for these fish. Catfish pellets and tablets are also excellent.

Seuss Corydoras / *Corydoras seussi*

This is nearly identical to *C. gossei*, apart from the fact that this fish is found in Colombia and *C. seussi* is found in Brazil. In addition, when adult, *C. seussi* has a much more elongated snout. It is really only when the two fish are put side by side that the obvious difference can be seen. They have been imported and sold mistakenly for each other on many occasions. The best time to confirm which is which is when they are semi-adult.

ORIGIN
south america

TEMPERATURE RANGE
70–79°F (21–26°C)

COMMUNITY
excellent

ADULT SIZE
female 3 in (8cm)
male 3 in (8cm)

DIET
all foods

EASE OF KEEPING
9/10

PH RANGE
6.8–7.5

Feeding

They will take all types of food, but thrive on a wide variety of flakes, frozen and live foods. Live foods such as bloodworm, daphnia, glassworm and tubifex are very good for these fish. Catfish pellets and tablets are also excellent.

Pigmy Corydoras / *Corydoras pygmaeus*

This fish will swim in all areas of the tank and is quite hardy. They are always on the move seemingly looking for food. They also like to perch on the leaves of the plants in your aquarium and seem to watch over everything that is going on in your tank. When your dealer has them for sale, they are rarely larger than about $1/2$ in (1.5cm) but they are quite cheap to buy and so a small shoal is not expensive. A sand base is by far the best substrate to keep this fish on. They are very hardy and so easy to keep and maintain.

Feeding

They will take all types of food, but thrive on a wide variety of flakes, frozen and live foods. Live foods such as bloodworm, daphnia, glassworm and tubifex are very good for these fish. Catfish pellets and tablets are also excellent.

ORIGIN
south america

TEMPERATURE RANGE
70–79°F (21–26°C)

COMMUNITY
excellent

ADULT SIZE
female 1 in (2.5cm)
male 1 in (2.5cm)

DIET
all foods

EASE OF KEEPING
9/10

PH RANGE
6.8–7.5

CATFISH

Snowflake Bristlenose / *Ancistrus hoplogenys*

ORIGIN
south america

TEMPERATURE RANGE
70–79°F (22–26°C)

COMMUNITY
excellent

ADULT SIZE
female 6 in (15cm)
male 6 in (15cm)

DIET
all foods

EASE OF KEEPING
10/10

PH RANGE
6.8–7.5

There are a small number of other fish very similar to this that are incorrectly called by the same name. The fish in this photograph is the real one. It has very fine white spots the size of a pinhead and white bars edging the dorsal fin and the tail, while those that are wrongly named have larger spots and only one white bar. The difference between male and female is that the male has soft bristles all over its snout and head region, and the female only has small bristles around the edge of the chin area. With a rasping, under-slung mouth they will graze all over the glass and any rocks searching for algae.

Feeding

They will take all types of food, but thrive on a wide variety of flakes, frozen and live foods. Live foods such as bloodworm, daphnia, glassworm and tubifex are very good for these fish. Catfish pellets and tablets are also excellent.

Albino Pangassius or Shark Catfish /

Pangassius sutchi "Albino"

This fish grows to an extremely large size in the wild. In most home aquariums they only tend to reach about 10 in (25cm), which is still very big. The mouth is very wide and deep and, if they are underfed, you will find the other inhabitants of your aquarium disappearing. They are certainly not community fish. They are constantly on the move in the aquarium, seemingly unable to settle and rest, and because of this similarity to the shark they were given their common name of Shark catfish. They are what is known as a 'naked fish', that is they have no scales. As a result, they can be difficult to treat with some medications if you have a problem with them.

Feeding

They will take all types of food, but thrive on a wide variety of flakes, frozen and live foods. Live foods such as bloodworm, daphnia, glassworm and tubifex are very good for these fish. Catfish pellets and tablets are also excellent.

ORIGIN
asia

TEMPERATURE RANGE
71.5–79°F (22–26°C)

COMMUNITY
only with larger fish

ADULT SIZE
female 40 in (100cm)
male 40 in (100cm)

DIET
all foods

EASE OF KEEPING
8/10

PH RANGE
6.8–7.5

Banjo Catfish / *Bunocephalus coracoideus*

ORIGIN
asia

TEMPERATURE RANGE
70–79°F (21–26°C)

COMMUNITY
excellent

ADULT SIZE
female 6 in (15cm)
male 6 in (15cm)

DIET
all foods

EASE OF KEEPING
10/10

PH RANGE
6.8–7.5

The Banjo catfish is a really unusual looking fish. They are very flat bodied; this is mainly because they like to bury into the substrate of their surroundings. If possible, they prefer a sand-based substrate. Using sand makes under-gravel filtration very difficult, so it is advisable to use a good external power filter. Although this fish is quite tolerant of water quality, it prefers good filtration. They will not swim after live food, preferring to forage through the substrate.

Feeding
They will take all types of food, but thrive on a wide variety of frozen and live foods. Live foods such as bloodworm and tubifex are very good for these fish. Catfish pellets and tablets are also excellent.

CATFISH

Black Lancer / *Bagroides macracanthus*

ORIGIN
asia

TEMPERATURE RANGE
70–79°F (21–26°C)

COMMUNITY
only with larger fish

ADULT SIZE
female 13 ³/₄ in (35cm)
male 13 ³/₄ in (35cm)

DIET
all foods

EASE OF KEEPING
9/10

PH RANGE
6.8–7.5

When fully settled in the aquarium, this fish has a dark brown to black body with a thin white line running through the centre and white edging to the tail. It is normally a nocturnal fish, only coming out of its hiding area to feed. They are usually available in an aquarium shop at about 4 in (10cm) and are not expensive. They need rockwork in the aquarium to create caves in which to hide or, alternatively, plenty of plants. Be careful when handling them because the dorsal fin and the pectoral fins have very sharp spines.

Feeding

They will take all types of food, but thrive on a wide variety of flakes, frozen and live foods. Live foods such as bloodworm, daphnia, glassworm and tubifex are very good for these fish. Catfish pellets and tablets are also excellent.

Frog Mouthed Catfish / *Chaca chaca*

Many people buy this fish because it is so ugly and seems to just lie on the bottom of the aquarium doing nothing. Do not be misled by this. Its mouth is very oversized for the size of this fish. If it is hungry, anything that it can catch and get into its mouth it will eat. In the wild, the fish will lie in amongst the mulm on the bottom of a stream or river until night and then go looking for food. They are not the best of swimmers. Larger fish are in no danger from it.

ORIGIN
asia

TEMPERATURE RANGE
70–79°F (21–26°C)

COMMUNITY
only with larger fish

ADULT SIZE
female 8 in (20cm)
male 8 in (20cm)

DIET
all foods

EASE OF KEEPING
9/10

PH RANGE
6.8 – 7.5

Feeding

They will take all types of food, but thrive on a wide variety of frozen and live foods. Live foods such as bloodworm and tubifex are very good for these fish. Catfish pellets and tablets are also excellent.

Debauwi Catfish / *Etropielus debauwi*

As with a number of other catfish, this is a 'naked fish', which makes for a slightly different approach to treating ailments such as white spot. The best way to handle this is to increase the temperature to about 30 degrees for a period of 24 hours and then reset the thermostat. Let the water cool down by itself and hopefully the problem should be solved. They are a mid-water swimmer and prefer to be in a shoal of about six or more. Do not keep really small fish in the same aquarium.

Feeding

They will take all types of food, but thrive on a wide variety of flakes, frozen and live foods. Live foods such as bloodworm, daphnia, glassworm and tubifex are very good for these fish. Catfish pellets and tablets are also excellent.

ORIGIN
africa

TEMPERATURE RANGE
70–79°F (21–26°C)

COMMUNITY
with medium or larger
fish

ADULT SIZE
female 3 ¹/₂ in (9cm)
male 3 ¹/₂ in (9cm)

DIET
all foods

EASE OF KEEPING
8/10

PH RANGE
6.8–7.5

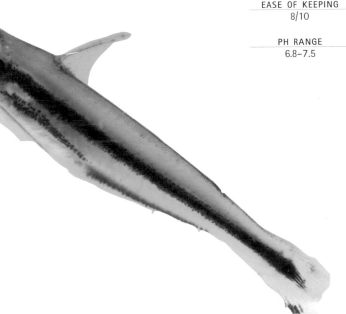

CATFISH

Flagtail Dianema / *Dianema urostriata*

ORIGIN
south america

TEMPERATURE RANGE
71.5–79°F (22–26°C)

COMMUNITY
very good

ADULT SIZE
female 5 in (13cm)
male 5 in (13cm)

DIET
all foods

EASE OF KEEPING
9/10

PH RANGE
6.8–7.5

Unusually for catfish, this is a bubble-nest breeder. This fish has been observed breeding in the wild but not, as yet, in the home aquarium. They like to have a well-planted aquarium with plenty of broad-leafed plants to lie on and also some darker, shaded areas to rest in. In a very brightly lit aquarium, they will generally only come out of hiding as the light goes down. They will also come to the surface from time to time and take in large mouthfuls of air.

Feeding

They will take all types of food, but thrive on a wide variety of flakes, frozen and live foods. Live foods such as bloodworm, daphnia, glassworm and tubifex are very good for these fish. Catfish pellets and tablets are also excellent.

L17 Flathead Ancistrus / *L017 Pseudoancistrus sp.*

CATFISH

Because so many new species of catfish have been found in recent years, many of them have not been truly classified and named as yet. Consequently, a coding system has been established to give them a basic identity until such time as the work is done on these fish. You will see fish now known as 'L' numbers and 'LDA' numbers. There are approximately 400 species in this category. This one has a very compressed body with large, striking pectorals. It also has a large, fleshy under-slung mouth with which to rasp over and chew its food. Sexual differences are not known at this time.

ORIGIN
south america

TEMPERATURE RANGE
71.5–79°F (22–26°C)

COMMUNITY
excellent

ADULT SIZE
female 8 in (20cm)
male 8 in (20cm)

DIET
all foods

EASE OF KEEPING
10/10

PH RANGE
6.5–7.2

Feeding

They will take all types of food, but thrive on a wide variety of flakes, frozen and live foods. Live foods such as bloodworm and tubifex are very good for these fish. Foods such cut green beans are also good for them. Catfish pellets and tablets are excellent.

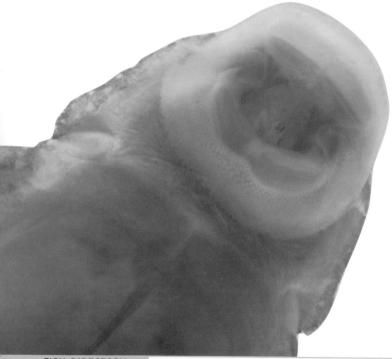

L27 Royal Pleco / *L027 Panaque nigrolineatus*

There are basically three colour varieties of this fish and quite a few location varieties of each of the colours. Supply of this fish is quite patchy so it is advisable to buy when you see them. They will require bogwood in the aquarium as they like to rasp tiny pieces from it and eat it, which aids their digestion. They also relish cut green beans. With their high back and multitude of stripes, they make a very attractive addition to your aquarium. As they become adult, the top and bottom rays of the tail become extended to form whip-like appendages. When handling this fish, do not allow your fingers to get trapped between the pectoral fins and the body as this can be quite painful.

Feeding

They will take all types of food, but thrive on a wide variety of flakes, frozen and live foods. Live foods such as bloodworm and tubifex are very good for these fish. A 1-in (2.5-cm) cube of raw potato is also good for them. Catfish pellets and tablets are excellent.

ORIGIN
south america

TEMPERATURE RANGE
71.5–79°F (22–26°C)

COMMUNITY
excellent

ADULT SIZE
female 10 in (25cm)
male 10 in (25cm)

DIET
all foods

EASE OF KEEPING
10/10

PH RANGE
6.5–7.2

L28 Angel Pleco / *L028 Hypancistrus sp.*

ORIGIN
south america

TEMPERATURE RANGE
71.5–79°F (22–26°C)

COMMUNITY
excellent

ADULT SIZE
female 10 in (25cm)
male 10 in (25cm)

DIET
all foods

EASE OF KEEPING
10/10

PH RANGE
6.5–7.2

Normally, when these fish are available, they are about 2–3 ¾ in (6–9.5cm) in length. They will settle into your aquarium very easily. Their colour is generally a mottled effect of light and dark brown with bright white spots, which are all over the body and fins. As with many varieties of this type of catfish, they grow to a good size, and the only danger to other fish in your aquarium is being pushed out of the way if these fish decide they want to be somewhere. Plants in your aquarium need to be of the larger, stronger varieties, otherwise they will be dislodged from the substrate and ruined.

Feeding

They will take all types of food, but thrive on a wide variety of flakes, frozen and live foods. Live foods such as bloodworm and tubifex are very good for these fish. A few cut green beans are good for them also. Catfish pellets and tablets are excellent.

L37 Honeycomb Pleco / *L037 Hypostomus sp.*

Many of this type of fish are available on a regular basis, although this variety is fairly rare. As you can see from the photograph, they have an attractive golden brown body colour with thin lines marking out a honeycomb pattern. When these fish are juveniles the patterning is only on the head area. As they grow, the pattern progresses further back, eventually covering the whole body. The dorsal fin is more like a sail and is relatively large compared with the size of the body. They will also 'stand' on their pectorals as if they are showing off to the other fish in your aquarium.

ORIGIN
south america

TEMPERATURE RANGE
71.5–79°F (22–26°C)

COMMUNITY
excellent

ADULT SIZE
female 10 in (25cm)
male 10 in (25cm)

DIET
all foods

EASE OF KEEPING
10/10

PH RANGE
6.5–7.2

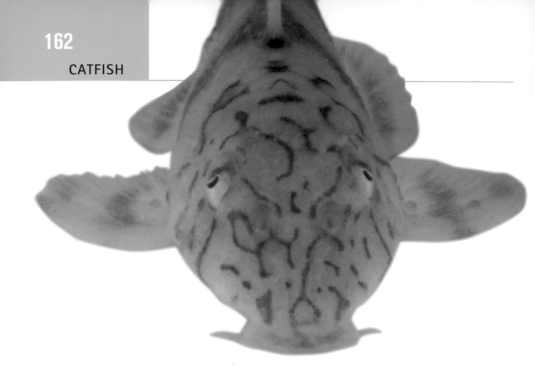

Feeding

They will take all types of food, but thrive on a wide variety of flakes, frozen and live foods. Live foods such as bloodworm and tubifex are very good for these fish. A few cut green beans are also good for them. Catfish pellets and tablets are excellent.

L47 Magnum Pleco / *L047 Baryancistrus sp.*

The Magnum pleco is regularly available and is very popular with fish-keepers. The body colouration normally ranges from olive grey to olive green. On the dorsal fin and the tail, there is a white bar on the edge that is yellowy white to bright yellow. This can also be seen on the pectoral and ventral fins of some specimens, depending on the original location of the fish.

Feeding

They will take all types of food, but thrive on a wide variety of flakes, frozen and live foods. Live foods such as bloodworm and tubifex are very good for these fish. A few cut green beans and a small piece of raw potato are also good for them. Catfish pellets and tablets are excellent.

ORIGIN
south america

TEMPERATURE RANGE
71.5–79°F (22–26°C)

COMMUNITY
excellent

ADULT SIZE
female 10 in (25cm)
male 10 in (25cm)

DIET
all foods

EASE OF KEEPING
10/10

PH RANGE
6.5–7.2

Feeding

They will take all types of food, but thrive on a wide variety of flakes, frozen and live foods. Live foods such as bloodworm and tubifex are very good for these fish. A few cut green beans and a small piece of raw potato are also good for them. Catfish pellets and tablets are excellent.

L50 Royal Pleco / *L050 Cochliodon sp.*

When growing from juvenile into semi-adulthood this fish develops what looks like a pointed lump on top of its head. As the fish grows, the lump becomes even more pronounced. The fish eventually looks as if it has a very high head shape running into its back. The body colouration is pale brown and the fins have reddish brown wide bars running through them. The spots on the body vary from fish to fish. Some have a few small black spots while other specimens have fewer but much larger spots. No two fish are totally identical.

Feeding

They will take all types of food, but thrive on a wide variety of flakes, frozen and live foods. Live foods such as bloodworm and tubifex are very good for these fish. A 1-in (2.5-cm) cube of raw potato is also good for them. Catfish pellets and tablets are excellent.

ORIGIN
south america

TEMPERATURE RANGE
71.5–79°F (22–26°C)

COMMUNITY
excellent

ADULT SIZE
female 5 $^3/_4$ in (15cm)
male 5 $^3/_4$ in (15cm)

DIET
all foods

EASE OF KEEPING
10/10

PH RANGE
6.5–7.2

CATFISH

L56 Chubby Pleco / *L056 Ancistrinae gen sp.*

ORIGIN
south america

TEMPERATURE RANGE
71.5–79°F (22–26°C)

COMMUNITY
Excellent

ADULT SIZE
female 5 ³/₄ in (15cm)
male 5 ³/₄ in (15cm)

DIET
all foods

EASE OF KEEPING
10/10

PH RANGE
6.5–7.2

The colouration varies on this fish from charcoal grey to jet-black. The pectoral fins, as with most of the other 'pleco' varieties, are extremely strong, so do not get your fingers trapped. On the leading edge of the first ray of the pectoral fin are very small stiff bristles and also at the bottom of the gill opening area you will see a cluster of bristles that are like spikes. On the male these bristles are generally quite long, up to 1 in (2.5cm) and on the females they are very short. They are normally folded back against the body until you attempt to lift the fish out of the aquarium. Bogwood in the aquarium is a must for these fish.

Feeding

They will take all types of food, but thrive on a wide variety of flakes, frozen and live foods. Live foods such as bloodworm and tubifex are very good for these fish. A 1-inch (2.5cm) cube of raw potato is also good for them and they will benefit from cut green beans. Catfish pellets and tablets are excellent.

L90 Papa Panaque / *L090 Panaque sp.*

There are two different pattern types of this fish. The fish in the photograph has a reticulated pattern all over the body. Most of the tail is clear, with a black bar running down the edge at the end of the tail. As the fish becomes adult, the top and bottom rays of the tail become greatly extended with long filaments. The other variety has a charcoal-coloured body and a bright white bar running up the caudal peduncle and across the top of the tail, with the remainder of the tail being black. They also grow extensions on the tail but they are bright white. This is quite a hardy fish.

Feeding

They will take all types of food, but thrive on a wide variety of flakes, frozen and live foods. Live foods such as bloodworm and tubifex are very good for these fish. A 1-inch (2.5cm) cube of raw potato is also good for them and catfish pellets and tablets are excellent.

ORIGIN
south america

TEMPERATURE RANGE
71.5–79°F (22–26°C)

COMMUNITY
excellent

ADULT SIZE
female 10 in (25cm)
male 10 in (25cm)

DIET
all foods

EASE OF KEEPING
10/10

PH RANGE
6.5–7.2

L102 Snowball Pleco / *L102 Hypancistrus sp.*

ORIGIN
south america

TEMPERATURE RANGE
71.5–79°F (22–26°C)

COMMUNITY
excellent

ADULT SIZE
female 7 in (18cm)
male 7 in (18cm)

DIET
all foods

EASE OF KEEPING
10/10

PH RANGE
6.5–7.2

The body pattern and colouration on this fish are extremely variable. They range from a mottled, dark brown to a black body with greyish patches. The spots also vary greatly with some fish having very small spots while others have large spots. There are no two identical patterned fish. They have a sail-like dorsal fin and tail. As with most of the other varieties, this fish also has a very soft, fleshy under-slung mouth, which it uses to rasp and graze over all the surfaces in the aquarium looking for food.

Feeding

They will take all types of food, but thrive on a wide variety of flakes, frozen and live foods. Live foods such as bloodworm and tubifex are very good for these fish. This fish relishes cut green beans. Catfish pellets and tablets are also excellent.

L114 Leopard Cactus Pleco /
L114 Pseudacanthicus leopardus.

The fish we have here is a juvenile and is only about 3 ¾ in (9.5cm) in length. As this fish becomes adult, the colouration in the tail changes to the same colour and pattern as the rest of the body. The reticulated body pattern also becomes finer. The first ray of the dorsal fin, the top and bottom ray of the tail and the first ray of the pectoral fins are extremely rigid and bone-like. When lifted from the water, the dorsal and pectoral fins lock in position and will not move unless the fish wants to move them. You would have to break them to make them move.

Feeding

They will take all types of food, but thrive on a wide variety of flakes, frozen and live foods. Live foods such as bloodworm and tubifex are very good for these fish. They like cut green beans but are also very partial to whole cockles and mussels. Catfish pellets and tablets are also excellent.

ORIGIN
south america

TEMPERATURE RANGE
71.5–79°F (22–26°C)

COMMUNITY
excellent

ADULT SIZE
female 10 in (25cm)
male 10 in (25cm)

DIET
all foods

EASE OF KEEPING
10/10

PH RANGE
6.5–7.2

CATFISH | **L128 Blue Phantom** / *L128 Ancistrinae gen sp.*

ORIGIN
south america

TEMPERATURE RANGE
71.5–79°F (22–26°C)

COMMUNITY
excellent

ADULT SIZE
female 8 in (20cm)
male 8 in (20cm)

DIET
all foods

EASE OF KEEPING
10/10

PH RANGE
6.5–7.2

Unfortunately, we do not see this fish very often. Whenever they are available they are purchased very quickly, as they are extremely popular. The body and fins are usually olive green and covered all over with small spots, except for the tail. On some specimens there is a white edging to the dorsal fin and the tail. Some fish also have a jade blue colour on the rear half of the body, as well as on the dorsal and tail fins. If you look on the front lip of the mouth, you will see a row of soft flexible teeth, which it uses to grate and break down solid foods. These teeth cannot hurt you.

Feeding
They will take all types of food, but thrive on a wide variety of flakes, frozen and live foods. Live foods such as bloodworm and tubifex are very good for these fish. They like cut green beans but are also very partial to whole cockles and mussels. Catfish pellets and tablets are also excellent.

L137 Bruno Cochliodon / *L137 Cochliodon sp.*

Many aquarium shops do not stock this fish because they think its colouration is too plain However, the opposite is true in this case. The body and fins have a reddish brown hue and the large-scale lines are very enhanced. It develops a high back as it grows into an adult. The dorsal fin also becomes sail-like, with a few very thick rays. There is also a beautiful steel-blue ring around its eyes. The mouth has two sets of flexible teeth, which it uses to great effect. It is advisable to have plenty of bogwood in your aquarium for this fish to rasp on.

Feeding

They will take all types of food, but thrive on a wide variety of flakes, frozen and live foods. Live foods such as bloodworm and tubifex are very good for these fish. A 1-in (2.5-cm) cube of raw potato is good for them. Catfish pellets and tablets are also excellent.

ORIGIN
south america

TEMPERATURE RANGE
71.5–79°F (22–26°C)

COMMUNITY
excellent

ADULT SIZE
female 8 in (20cm)
male 8 in (20cm)

DIET
all foods

EASE OF KEEPING
10/10

PH RANGE
6.5–7.2

CATFISH

L333 / *L333 Hypancistrus sp.*

ORIGIN
south america

TEMPERATURE RANGE
71.5–79°F (22–26°C)

COMMUNITY
excellent

ADULT SIZE
female 5 ³/₄ in (15cm)
male 5 ³/₄ in (15cm)

DIET
all foods

EASE OF KEEPING
10/10

PH RANGE
6.5–7.2

This is one of the very latest fish that have become available from Brazil and they have already proved to be very popular. From the little we know about this fish, they are extremely easy to keep and with the very fine black and white scribbled patterning on the body will be an attraction that no fish-keeper will want to miss out on. The sexing and breeding of this fish are as yet unknown. They can quite happily be put in with very small, free-swimming fish without any problem.

Feeding

They will take all types of food, but thrive on a wide variety of flakes, frozen and live foods. Live foods such as bloodworm and tubifex are very good for these fish. A 1-in (2.5-cm) cube of raw potato is also good for them. In addition, cut green beans, catfish pellets and tablets are excellent.

LDA1 Gold Stripe Panaque / *LDA1Panaque sp.*

One of the smaller Panaque sp., it grows to around 3 ¾ in (9.5cm). Because of its small adult size, it is extremely popular with all fish-keepers. It is a very attractive fish with chocolate brown and cream stripes running across the body and fins and also up the head. They are normally available in aquarium shops at around 1 ½–2 in (4–5cm) and are not overly expensive. They are very hardy and easy to keep. Good water conditions are required but regular water changes should be sufficient to maintain this.

Feeding

They will take all types of food, but thrive on a wide variety of flakes, frozen and live foods. Live foods such as bloodworm and tubifex are very good for these fish. Cut green beans in small amounts are also good and catfish pellets and tablets are excellent.

ORIGIN
south america

TEMPERATURE RANGE
71.5–79°F (22–26°C)

COMMUNITY
excellent

ADULT SIZE
female 3 ³/₄ in (9.5cm)
male 3 ³/₄ in (9.5cm)

DIET
all foods

EASE OF KEEPING
10/10

PH RANGE
6.5 – 7.2

Blue Pangassius or Shark Catfish / *Pangassius sutchi*

ORIGIN
asia

TEMPERATURE RANGE
71.5–79°F (22–26°C)

COMMUNITY
only with larger fish

ADULT SIZE
female 40 in (100cm)
male 40 in (100cm)

DIET
all foods

EASE OF KEEPING
8/10

PH RANGE
6.8–7.5

This fish grows to an extremely large size in the wild. In most home aquariums they only tend to get to about 10 in (25cm), which is still very big. The mouth is very wide and deep and, if they are underfed, you will find the other inhabitants of your aquarium disappearing. They are certainly not a community fish. They are constantly on the move in the aquarium, seemingly unable to settle and rest, hence their similarity to the shark and their common name of Shark catfish. They are what is known as a 'naked fish', because they have no scales. As a result, they can be difficult to treat with some medications if you have a problem with them.

Feeding

They will take all types of food, but thrive on a wide variety of flakes, frozen and live foods. Live foods such as bloodworm, daphnia, glassworm and tubifex are very good for these fish. Catfish pellets and tablets are also excellent.

Angelicus Pimelodus / *Pimelodus pictus*

Also known as the Pim Pictus, this fish is always very active, swimming in all areas of the aquarium. The mouth is very wide, so it is advisable not to put fish such neons or Cardinal tetra-sized fish in with them. Fish the size of platies or swordtails are generally okay. Keeping more than one of these in your aquarium is not a problem. However, you will find that, although they will not damage each other, they will be the first to the food and will squabble with each other over it. The sexing and breeding habits of this fish are unknown.

Feeding

They will take all types of food, but thrive on a wide variety of flakes, frozen and live foods. Live foods such as bloodworm, daphnia, glassworm and tubifex are very good for these fish. Catfish pellets and tablets are also excellent.

ORIGIN
south america

TEMPERATURE RANGE
71.5–79°F (22–26°C)

COMMUNITY
good with medium to
larger fish only.

ADULT SIZE
female 5 ³/₄ in (15cm)
male 5 ³/₄ in (15cm)

DIET
all foods

EASE OF KEEPING
8/10

PH RANGE
6.5–7.2

Spotted Bullnose / *Chaetostoma sp.*

ORIGIN
south america

TEMPERATURE RANGE
71.5–79°F (22–26°C)

COMMUNITY
excellent

ADULT SIZE
female 4 ³/₄ in (12cm)
male 4 ³/₄ in (12cm)

DIET
all foods

EASE OF KEEPING
9/10

PH RANGE
6.5–7.2

There are a small number of different species of this fish available but generally it is only the standard bullnose or the spotted bullnose that are available. The body is normally a solid slate-grey colouration but this can vary with different shadings. There are large black spots all over the body and head, and the chin area has much more flesh than normal. It is like having an extra thick lip at the front end. They like to have places where they can hide away, so rockwork and bogwood is advisable.

Feeding
They will take all types of food, but thrive on a wide variety of flakes, frozen and live foods. Live foods such as bloodworm and tubifex are very good for these fish. Cut green beans in small quantities are also good for them. Catfish pellets and tablets are excellent.

Long Nose Whiptail / *Sturisoma aureum*

Up until recently, this fish was only imported from the wild but they are being bred with great success in the Czech Republic. They are normally only available from there at about 3 ¹/₄–3 ¹/₂ in (8–9cm) but they are very strong and hardy. They grow very fine filament-like extensions to the tail, which can be as long as the body. These are very delicate, but if they break they will grow again These fish like to have plenty of fine-leafed plants in the aquarium to lie amongst. The head is very wide with a twig-like body. All of the fins look oversized for the shape of the body.

Feeding

They will take all types of food, but thrive on a wide variety of flakes, frozen and live foods. Live foods such as bloodworm and tubifex are very good for these fish. Cut green beans in small quantities are also good for them. Catfish pellets and tablets are excellent.

ORIGIN
south america

TEMPERATURE RANGE
71.5–79°F (22–26°C)

COMMUNITY
excellent

ADULT SIZE
female 10 in (25cm)
male 10 in (25cm)

DIET
all foods

EASE OF KEEPING
8/10

PH RANGE
6.5–7.2

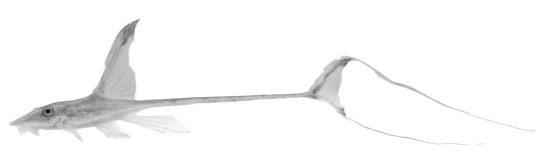

CATFISH

Cuckoo Synodontis / *Synodontis multipunctatus*

ORIGIN
africa

TEMPERATURE RANGE
71.5–79°F (22–26°C)

COMMUNITY
very good

ADULT SIZE
female 5 ³/₄ in (15cm)
male 5 ³/₄ in (15cm)

DIET
all foods

EASE OF KEEPING
8/10

PH RANGE
6.5–7.2

This is a very brightly marked fish with jet black and brilliant white colours on a silvery brown body. Although it is very rarely bred in captivity, it is known that breeding pairs will bully other fish that have just laid their eggs and force them to leave the area. The intruding Cuckoo synodontis fish then spawn, lay their own eggs in the same location and allow the original parent fish to return. The foster parent fish will then care for all the eggs until they have hatched and the fry have grown large enough to fend for themselves. The original parents have nothing to do with the youngsters at all. These fish really are the cuckoos of the fish world.

Feeding

They will take all types of food, but thrive on a wide variety of flakes, frozen and live foods. Live foods such as bloodworm and tubifex are very good for these fish. Catfish pellets and tablets are also excellent.

Vermiculated Synodontis / *Synodontis schoutendeni*

As with nearly all of the synodontis group of fish, the sexing and breeding habits are unknown. As you can see from the photographs of this fish, they like their food. The many barbels that they have are constantly used to 'feeling' for food in the substrate, so beware of overfeeding them. They are generally very active in the aquarium, although in the wild they normally only feed at night. Ensure that there is plenty of cover for them to hide in or under. Bogwood is the ideal plant as you can also use it for décor.

ORIGIN
africa

TEMPERATURE RANGE
71.5–79°F (22–26°C)

COMMUNITY
very good

ADULT SIZE
female 5 ³/₄ in (15cm)
male 5 ³/₄ in (15cm)

DIET
all foods

EASE OF KEEPING
8/10

PH RANGE
6.5–7.2

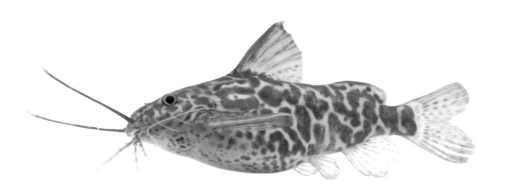

Feeding

They will take all types of food, but thrive on a wide variety of flakes, frozen and live foods. Live foods such as bloodworm and tubifex are very good for these fish. Catfish pellets and tablets are also excellent.

Zebra Otocinclus / *Otocinclus sp.*

This is a very new fish to the hobby, with the first specimens only coming available in 2002. When they are very small, the body pattern of this fish is mottled all over. However, as it grows older, this gradually changes to a striped pattern running from top to bottom of the body. They have a very small under-slung mouth, which they use to great effect to graze on any area in the aquarium where there is algae. When they are available, they are normally only about ¾ in (2cm) in length and are quite expensive, but they are a worthwhile addition to your aquarium.

ORIGIN
south america

TEMPERATURE RANGE
71.5–79°F (22–26°C)

COMMUNITY
excellent

ADULT SIZE
female 2 ½ in (6.5cm)
male 2 ½ in (6.5cm)

DIET
all foods

EASE OF KEEPING
10/10

PH RANGE
6.5–7.2

Feeding

They will take all types of food, but thrive on a wide variety of flakes, frozen and live foods. Live foods such as bloodworm and tubifex are very good for these fish. Cut green beans in small quantities are also good for them. Catfish pellets and tablets are excellent.

Black Kuhli Loach / *Acanthopthalmus sp.*

When placing this fish in your aquarium, ensure that there are no small gaps in the top as they are great escape artists. They will get out of the smallest of gaps and the next thing is you find them on the floor. There are a number of different types of Kuhli loach and you can keep them all together without any problem. The body gets no thicker than a pencil. They are very fast movers and so can be quite difficult to catch if you want to move them to another aquarium. If you keep several in your aquarium, you will normally find that when you turn the lights out at night, they will all stay together in their favourite place.

ORIGIN
asia

TEMPERATURE RANGE
72–79°F (22–26°C)

COMMUNITY
excellent

ADULT SIZE
female 4 in (10cm)
male 4 in (10cm)

DIET
all foods

EASE OF KEEPING
10/10

PH RANGE
6.8–7.5

Feeding

They will take all types of food, but thrive on a wide variety of flakes, frozen and live foods. Live foods such as bloodworm and tubifex are very good for these fish. Catfish pellets and tablets are also excellent.

Dario Loach / *Botia dario*

The Dario loach swims on and around the bottom of the aquarium most of the time. If you keep more than one of these, they will push each other around as they are looking for food. But they do no damage to each other, nor will they damage the other fish in your aquarium. They are a very attractive fish, with dark brown bars and thin yellow stripes running top to bottom of the body and yellow pectoral fins. When resting, they have a habit of sitting very high on their pectoral fins with their eyes seeming to look from left to right and back again.

Feeding

They will take all types of food, but thrive on a wide variety of flakes, frozen and live foods. Live foods such as bloodworm and tubifex are very good for these fish. Catfish pellets and tablets are also excellent.

ORIGIN
india (asia)

TEMPERATURE RANGE
70–79°F (21–26°C)

COMMUNITY
excellent

ADULT SIZE
female 3 1/4 in (8cm)
male 3 1/4 in (8cm)

DIET
all foods

EASE OF KEEPING
9/10

PH RANGE
6.8–7.5

Gold Sucking Loach / *Gyrinochielus aymonieri*

ORIGIN
asia

TEMPERATURE RANGE
66–79°F (19–26°C)

COMMUNITY
only with larger fish

ADULT SIZE
female 10 in (25cm)
male 10 in (25cm)

DIET
all foods

EASE OF KEEPING
9/10

PH RANGE
6.8–7.5

As a result of this fish's sucker mouth, they will attach themselves to any surface in the aquarium, grazing for food. Unfortunately, this also includes the other inhabitants of your aquarium. If they attach themselves to the body of a smaller fish, they will do damage to the mucus covering that protects the fish, which will encourage disease. When they are small they are not too much of a problem, but once they get to about 3-4 in (8-10cm) they will do this more and more. If they are in the company of larger fish, they will just get shaken off when they try to attach themselves.

Feeding

They will take all types of food, but thrive on a wide variety of flakes, frozen and live foods. Live foods such as bloodworm and tubifex are very good for these fish. Algae flakes, catfish pellets and tablets are also excellent.

Red Finned Loach / *Botia lecontei*

This fish will occupy the bottom of the aquarium most of the time. It will mostly have its nose into the substrate looking for food. It is an attractive fish with a slate-grey body and bright orange to red fins. It is very similar to another botia but, when it is fully settled into your aquarium and in top condition, it differs by having a grey-green body. Being a 'naked fish', that is a fish without scales, they can be a little difficult to treat in the event of white spot or fungal problems. Increasing the temperature is normally the answer to this.

Feeding

They will take all types of food, but thrive on a wide variety of flakes, frozen and live foods. Live foods such as bloodworm and tubifex are very good for these fish. Algae flakes, catfish pellets and tablets are also excellent.

ORIGIN
asia

TEMPERATURE RANGE
73–80.5°F (23–27°C)

COMMUNITY
good

ADULT SIZE
female 5 ³/₄ in (15cm)
male 5 ³/₄ in (15cm)

DIET
all foods

EASE OF KEEPING
8/10

PH RANGE
6.8–7.5

Horae's Loach / *Botia morleti*

ORIGIN
asia

TEMPERATURE RANGE
73–82°F (23–28°C)

COMMUNITY
very good

ADULT SIZE
female 3 ³/₄ in (9.5cm)
male 3 ³/₄ in (9.5cm)

DIET
all foods

EASE OF KEEPING
8/10

PH RANGE
6.8–7.5

Again, this fish will occupy the bottom of the aquarium most of the time. It will have its nose in the substrate looking for food. This is a very attractive fish with a creamy beige body, black bar at the caudal peduncle and a black line running the length of the crown of the back. They like to have plenty of cover and hideaways in the aquarium. But once they are settled and established, they are usually very active during the day and only hide away at night. They will do better in your aquarium if you keep three or four of them together.

Feeding
They will take all types of food, but thrive on a wide variety of flakes, frozen and live foods. Live foods such as bloodworm and tubifex are very good for these fish. Algae flakes, catfish pellets and tablets are also excellent.

Dojo or Weather Loach / *Misgurnis anguillcaudatus*

Again, this fish will occupy the bottom of the aquarium most of the time but will swim up and down the glass. Having originated from China and Siberia, they will take very cool temperatures. However, they will also accept the higher temperatures in your aquarium and normally your supplier will have acclimatised them. They are very prone to fungal problems and this is difficult to treat but once settled they are not normally a problem. If you keep a shoal of four or five, it will help them to settle. There is also a spotted variety of this fish available.

Feeding
They will take all types of food, but thrive on a wide variety of flakes, frozen and live foods. Live foods such as bloodworm and tubifex are very good for these fish. Algae flakes, catfish pellets and tablets are also excellent.

ORIGIN
asia

TEMPERATURE RANGE
64–82°F (18–28°C)

COMMUNITY
very good

ADULT SIZE
female 12 in (30cm)
male 12 in (30cm)

DIET
all foods

EASE OF KEEPING
8/10

PH RANGE
6.8–7.5

Tiger Loach / *Botia berdmorei*

ORIGIN
asia

TEMPERATURE RANGE
70–79°F (21–26°C)

COMMUNITY
only with larger fish

ADULT SIZE
female 10 in (25cm)
male 10 in (25cm)

DIET
all foods

EASE OF KEEPING
9/10

PH RANGE
6.8–7.5

As you can see from the photographs, this fish has a long pointed snout, which it uses to great effect burrowing into the substrate looking for food. Its potentially large size can cause a problem because it will move the substrate everywhere except where you wanted it. It will unintentionally also uproot all the plants that you may have in your aquarium. Be careful not to have too many rocks or stones piled on top of each other as part of your tank decoration because they could fall over and damage the aquarium. Even though this fish grows to a large size, they are a worthwhile addition to your aquarium.

Feeding

They will take all types of food, but thrive on a wide variety of flakes, frozen and live foods. Live foods such as bloodworm and tubifex are very good for these fish. Algae flakes, catfish pellets and tablets are also excellent.

Manchurian Loach / *Leptobotia mantschurica*

This fish prefers cooler temperatures in your aquarium as it originates from very cool streams and rivers. With their long, tubular-shaped body and pointed snout, they need a good depth of substrate, as they will burrow into it quite deeply looking for food. The male has a spine under the eye which is very sharp, so be careful when handling this fish. Their breeding habits are unknown. When this fish is in top condition and fully settled, a faded blue area will develop behind the eye and the tail will have a strong yellow colouration in its opaque areas.

Feeding

They will take all types of food, but thrive on a wide variety of flakes, frozen and live foods. Live foods such as bloodworm and tubifex are very good for these fish. Algae flakes, catfish pellets and tablets are also excellent.

ORIGIN
russia/china (asia)

TEMPERATURE RANGE
64–75°F (18–24°C)

COMMUNITY
only with larger fish

ADULT SIZE
female 8 in (20cm)
male 8 in (20cm)

DIET
all foods

EASE OF KEEPING
9/10

PH RANGE
6.8–7.5

RAINBOWS

Black Line Rainbowfish / *Melanotaenia nigrans*

ORIGIN
papua new guinea

TEMPERATURE RANGE
66–75°C (19–24°C)

COMMUNITY
excellent

ADULT SIZE
female 3 in (8cm)
male 3 in (8cm)

DIET
all foods

EASE OF KEEPING
9/10

PH RANGE
6.8–7.5

Acquiring fish from Papua New Guinea has been very difficult, so a lot of work has gone into learning how to breed and raise these fish. Within the original specimens obtained were a number of local variations of this species and so you will see slightly different patterns and colourations of this fish available in aquarium shops. Although originating from a tropical area they prefer slightly cooler temperatures, if possible. They will react quite badly to high temperature in your aquarium, so try to avoid this by checking and maintaining your heater thermostat. The male has black edges to the dorsal and anal fins and, if you are successful in breeding these fish, you will find that they are egg-scatterers.

Feeding

They will take all types of food, but thrive on a wide variety of flakes, frozen and live foods. Live foods such as bloodworm, daphnia, glassworm and tubifex are very good for these fish.

Madagascar Rainbowfish / *Bedotia geayi*

This is a nice easy fish for the aquarium. They are quite hardy and very striking in their colouration. The body is a pale silvery colour, with the tail having a jet-black band edged with bright red. The posterior dorsal and the anal fins are black edged with orange to red colouration between the edging and the body. They are a schooling fish, swimming mainly in mid-water. The female is not quite as strongly coloured as the male and also has a rounded dorsal fin. They like to have plenty of fine-leafed plants in the aquarium and if they spawn will scatter their eggs in amongst the plant leaves.

Feeding

They will take all types of food, but thrive on a wide variety of flakes, frozen and live foods. Live foods such as bloodworm, daphnia, glassworm and tubifex are very good for these fish.

ORIGIN
madagascar

TEMPERATURE RANGE
68–77°F (20–25°C)

COMMUNITY
excellent

ADULT SIZE
female 5 in (13cm)
male 5 in (13cm)

DIET
all foods

EASE OF KEEPING
9/10

PH RANGE
6.8–7.5

Red Tail Rainbowfish / *Melanotaenia splendida australis*

ORIGIN
western australia

TEMPERATURE RANGE
71.5–80.5°F (22–27°C)

COMMUNITY
excellent

ADULT SIZE
female 5 in (13cm)
male 5 in (13cm)

DIET
all foods

EASE OF KEEPING
9/10

PH RANGE
6.8–7.5

This is another very nice, easy fish for the aquarium. They are extremely hardy and very striking in their colouration. The fish shown is a juvenile and as they become adult their colouration becomes really intense. The really light-coloured body, as seen here, changes to deep red scalation with a wide black bar running the length of the body behind this. The fins are also deep red with black edging. This fish is an egg-scatterer and so will need fine-leafed plants such as cabomba and myriophyllum. The female will swim into the plants, scattering the eggs, with the male following fertilising the eggs.

Feeding

They will take all types of food, but thrive on a wide variety of flakes, frozen and live foods. Live foods such as bloodworm, daphnia, glassworm and tubifex are very good for these fish.

Long Banded Rasbora / *Rasbora einthovenii*

RASBORAS

Rasboras come in many shapes and sizes and this is one of the elongated types. The eye is quite large compared to the body size. The body shape is designed to allow the fish to swim very fast, with power coming from its large tail. They are a shoaling fish and will do better if there are four or five together in the aquarium. When they are young, the markings and colouration are very untidy. As they grow, the scales become quite pronounced and the colours much stronger. In the event that you have disease problems with them, do not use any proprietary medication from your dealer that has copper in it.

Feeding

They will take all types of food, but thrive on a wide variety of flakes, frozen and live foods. Live foods such as bloodworm, daphnia, glassworm and tubifex are very good for these fish.

ORIGIN
asia

TEMPERATURE RANGE
71.5–79°F (22–26°C)

COMMUNITY
excellent

ADULT SIZE
female 3 ¹/₂ in (9cm)
male 3 ¹/₂ in (9cm)

DIET
all foods

EASE OF KEEPING
9/10

PH RANGE
6.8–7.5

Black Edged Rasbora / *Parluciosoma argyrotaenia*

ORIGIN
asia

TEMPERATURE RANGE
71.5–79°F (22–26°C)

COMMUNITY
excellent

ADULT SIZE
female 3 ³/₄ in (9.5cm)
male 3 ³/₄ in (9.5cm)

DIET
all foods

EASE OF KEEPING
9/10

PH RANGE
6.8–7.5

Again, this fish is one of the elongated variety and the eye is quite large compared to the body size. The streamlined body shape is designed to allow the fish to swim very fast, with power coming from its large tail. They are a shoaling fish and will do better if there are four or five together in your aquarium. As they grow into adults, the edges of the scales become quite pronounced with a black edging to them. A thick black line also becomes more distinguishable. In the event that you have disease problems with them, do not use any proprietary medication from your dealer that has copper in it.

Feeding

They will take all types of food, but thrive on a wide variety of flakes, frozen and live foods. Live foods such as bloodworm, daphnia, glassworm and tubifex are very good for these fish.

Pygmy Rasbora / *Rasbora brigittae*

This fish is totally different from the previous two as it is one of the pigmy group of rasboras. When available in an aquarium shop, they are rarely more that about $^1/_2$ in (1.5 cm) in length. To get any effect within your aquarium, you would need a shoal of at least 20. They are quite slow growing but when adult the male has a bright cherry-red hue all over its body with a reflective blue-black bar running through it. Plenty of fine-leafed plants are required for this fish in an aquarium. They are ideal to introduce to your aquarium after it has been running for about six months and is well established.

Feeding

They will take all types of food, but thrive on a wide variety of flakes, frozen and live foods. Live foods such as bloodworm, daphnia, glassworm and tubifex are very good for these fish.

ORIGIN
asia

TEMPERATURE RANGE
73–80.5°F (23–27°C)

COMMUNITY
excellent

ADULT SIZE
female 1 in (2.5cm)
male 1 in (2.5cm)

DIET
all foods

EASE OF KEEPING
9/10

PH RANGE
6.8–7.5

SHARKS

Harlequin Shark / *Labeo variegatus*

ORIGIN
zaire (africa)

TEMPERATURE RANGE
71.5–80.5°F (22–27°C)

COMMUNITY
very good with larger
fish

ADULT SIZE
female 12 in (30cm)
male 12 in (30cm)

DIET
all foods

EASE OF KEEPING
9/10

PH RANGE
6.8–7.5

You will need a large aquarium in which to keep and grow this fish. They are normally available from an aquarium dealer from about 2 ¾ in (7cm) upwards. They are a seasonal fish, only being available two or three times a year. They grow quite quickly and in the first year will grow 3 ¼–3 ½ in (8–9cm) very easily. Because of the way in which the fish moves so quickly around the bottom of the aquarium, it will be difficult to keep and grow any plants unless they were well-established, large-leafed, hardy ones that you planted before introducing this fish to your aquarium. A single fish is quite satisfactory.

Feeding

They will take all types of food, but thrive on a wide variety of flakes, frozen and live foods. Live foods such as bloodworm, daphnia, glassworm and tubifex are very good for these fish.

Silver Shark – Bala Shark /
Balantiochielus melanopterus

These fish are called sharks, because of their vague resemblance to real sharks. The body is silver with jet-black fringes to all the fins. It is a very attractive fish but you should be aware of its potential size. They will need a large aquarium to grow to their full size and also very good water quality. A high level of aeration is also required to help maintain this fish correctly. There are no known differences between male and female. They have been bred successfully in the Far East using hormones to trigger them into spawning and also using quite a number of fish in large ponds.

Feeding

They will take all types of food, but thrive on a wide variety of flakes, frozen and live foods. Live foods such as bloodworm, daphnia, glassworm and tubifex are very good for these fish.

ORIGIN
asia

TEMPERATURE RANGE
71.5–80.5°F (22–27°C)

COMMUNITY
very good with larger fish

ADULT SIZE
female 13 $^1/_2$ in (35cm)
male 13 $^1/_2$ in (35cm)

DIET
all foods

EASE OF KEEPING
9/10

PH RANGE
6.8–7.5

Four Eyes / *Anableps anableps*

ORIGIN
south america

TEMPERATURE RANGE
73–80.5°F (23–27°C)

COMMUNITY
good with larger fish

ADULT SIZE
female 12 in (30cm)
male 12 in (30cm)

DIET
all foods

EASE OF KEEPING
7/10

PH RANGE
6.8–7.5

This is a fish that could be classified as very unusual. They will normally swim at the surface of the water but they can see both above and below the water level at the same time because of their modified eyes. They originate from brackish water but can live in a non-brackish environment. They are a live-bearing fish and the male can be identified by the hardened ray on the anal fin, which is called the gonopodium. If you have too many in the aquarium, they will fight amongst themselves and can do damage to each other. They will jump and so a tight-fitting cover is required on your aquarium.

Feeding
They will take all types of food, but thrive on a wide variety of flakes, frozen and live foods. Live foods such as bloodworm, daphnia, glassworm and tubifex are very good for these fish. Freeze-dried foods that float such as mosquito larvae are also excellent.

Archer Fish / *Toxotes jaculator*

This is another fish that could be classified as very unusual. Again they will normally be seen swimming at the surface but this is because they have the ability to spit a jet of water at insects that are sitting on the leaves of plants above the surface. The jet of water knocks the insects into the water and the fish then immediately catches and eats them. These fish also originate from brackish water but can live in a non-brackish environment. They prefer slightly warmer water. If you keep them in a shoal, ensure that they are all about the same size otherwise there could be problems with fighting.

Feeding

They will take all types of food, but thrive on a wide variety of flakes, frozen and live foods. Live foods such as bloodworm, daphnia, glassworm and tubifex are very good for these fish. Freeze-dried foods that float such as mosquito larvae are also excellent.

ORIGIN
asia

TEMPERATURE RANGE
77–82°F (25–28°C)

COMMUNITY
good with larger fish

ADULT SIZE
female 8 in (20cm)
male 8 in (20cm)

DIET
all foods

EASE OF KEEPING
8/10

PH RANGE
6.8–7.5

Metallic Giradinus – Black Chin Livebearer /
Giradinus metallicus

ORIGIN
cuba (caribbean)

TEMPERATURE RANGE
70–75°F (21–24°C)

COMMUNITY
excellent

ADULT SIZE
female 3 in (8cm)
male 1 ½ in (4cm)

DIET
all foods

EASE OF KEEPING
9/10

PH RANGE
6.8–7.5

This live-bearer is unusual because the male is very small compared to the female. This type of fish is nearly always bred by private breeders. Extremely few come from the wild and these are nearly always collected by private expeditions and then introduced to existing brood stock to strengthen the bloodline. When keeping this fish, it is advisable to keep one male and three or four females together as a group. The female does not normally have more than 30-40 fry at a time. They are a very good community fish and quite hardy.

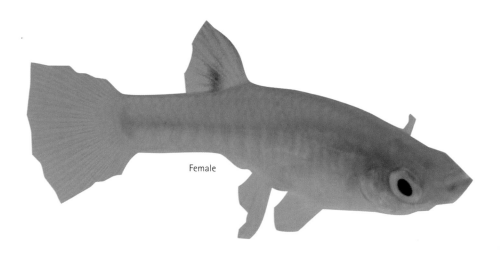

Female

Male

Feeding

They will take all types of food, but thrive on a wide variety of flakes,
frozen and live foods. Live foods such as bloodworm, daphnia, glassworm
and tubifex are very good for these fish. Freeze-dried foods that float
such as mosquito larvae are also excellent.

Borneo – Hong Kong Sucker / *Pseudogastromyzon sp*

ORIGIN
china (asia)

TEMPERATURE RANGE
64–79°F (18–26°C)

COMMUNITY
excellent

ADULT SIZE
female 4 in (10cm)
male 4 in (10cm)

DIET
all foods

EASE OF KEEPING
9/10

PH RANGE
6.8–7.5

Also known as the Butterfly pleco, this fish comes from very cold streams in China. It will, however, take the transference to warm water quite easily. This has to be done over a period of time, starting with cool water and day by day slightly increasing the temperature. This will generally take around 10 days to complete. There are a number of fish imported from China that are slightly different from this variety but all have the same name. There is still some confusion over the true identification of some of these fish. They will adhere to the glass of your aquarium very tightly, so be gentle when lifting them off the glass and only do so if you need to.

Feeding

They will take all types of food, but thrive on a wide variety of flakes, frozen and live foods. Live foods such as bloodworm, daphnia, glassworm and tubifex are very good for these fish.

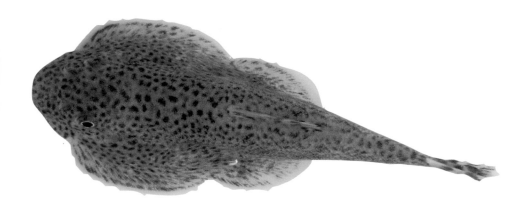

Butterfly Fish / *Pantodon bucholzi*

Another fish oddity – this one has the ability to 'fly' out of the water. The pectoral fins are exceptionally large in relation to the body and the fish use the fins to power their way out of the water. They can 'fly' for up to 6–10 ft (2–3m), so you must keep a tight-fitting cover on your aquarium. The lower jaw of the fish drops as they feed from the surface and the mouth becomes very large. Do not keep this fish with very small fish, such as tetras, as they will be eaten. They can take time to acclimatise to a new environment, so when you purchase them ensure that they are feeding without problem.

ORIGIN
africa

TEMPERATURE RANGE
71.5–82°F (22–28°C)

COMMUNITY
good with medium-
sized fish

ADULT SIZE
female 4 in (10cm)
male 4 in (10cm)

DIET
all foods

EASE OF KEEPING
8/10

PH RANGE
6.8–7.5

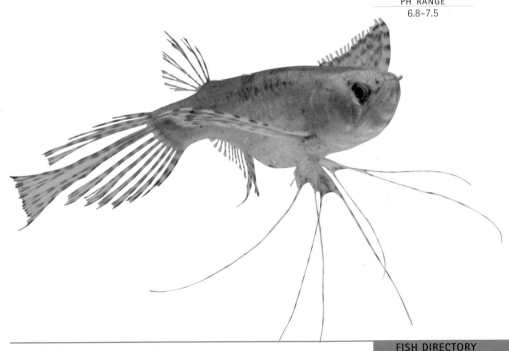

Feeding

They will take all types of food, but thrive on a wide variety of flakes, frozen and live foods. Live foods such as bloodworm, daphnia, glassworm and tubifex are very good for these fish. Freeze-dried foods that float such as mosquito larvae are also excellent.

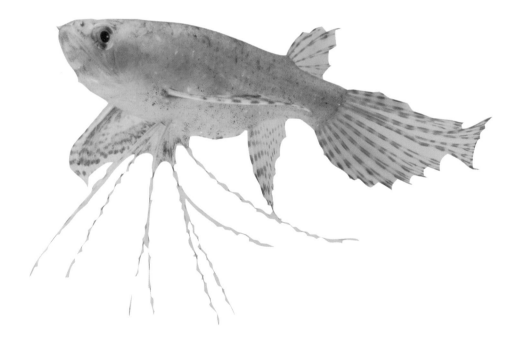

Celebes Halfbeak / *Nomorhamphus liemi*

Another fish oddity – this is because the upper part of the mouth is only half the size of the lower part. They belong to a group of fishes called 'Halfbeaks'. There are quite a few of them although, unfortunately, we do not see them very often. There are a couple of colour varieties of this fish and this particular one is being bred in captivity with great success in the Czech Republic. The males will 'fight' each other by locking their jaws together but no damage is done; it is just a test of strength to sort out which is the dominant male. They will nearly always swim in the upper half of your aquarium.

Feeding

They will take all types of food, but thrive on a wide variety of flakes, frozen and live foods. Live foods such as bloodworm, daphnia, glassworm and tubifex are very good for these fish. Freeze-dried foods that float such as mosquito larvae are also excellent.

ORIGIN
indonesia

TEMPERATURE RANGE
73–80.5°F (23–27°C)

COMMUNITY
good

ADULT SIZE
female 4 in (10cm)
male 4 in (10cm)

DIET
all foods

EASE OF KEEPING
9/10

PH RANGE
6.8–7.5

Fire Eel / *Mastacembelus erythrotaenia*

ORIGIN
asia

TEMPERATURE RANGE
73–80.5°F (23–27°C)

COMMUNITY
very good with larger
fish

ADULT SIZE
female 40 in (100cm)
male 40 in (100cm)

DIET
all foods

EASE OF KEEPING
9/10

PH RANGE
6.8–7.5

This fish is normally available in an aquarium shop at around 4–6 in (10-15cm) in length. When introduced into your aquarium, they will immediately swim to the bottom and, if possible, will go snout first into the substrate and completely bury themselves, with just the very tip of their snout showing. You will find that some of your plants do not stay anchored in the gravel for very long. Given time and patience, you can actually get this fish to accept food direct from your hand. It has no teeth, so it cannot bite you. As with all of this type of fish, ensure a tight-fitting cover is on your aquarium.

Feeding

They will take all types of food, but thrive on a wide variety of flakes, frozen and live foods. Live foods such as bloodworm, daphnia, glassworm and tubifex are very good for these fish. Grated beef heart is readily accepted.

Golden White Cloud Mountain Minnow /
Tanichthys albonubes "Gold"

This fish has been selectively bred by commercial breeders, who have also bred the standard White Cloud Mountain minnow. They noticed that about one fish in each brood was slightly different and then found another. Eventually, they bred these two types together and this fish is the end result. For all this inter-breeding, it is a very hardy fish and easy to maintain. They are quite expensive for what they are but this is because of the time and trouble taken to go through the selection process. Hopefully, as they become more freely available, the price will come down. It is best to keep them in a small shoal of 10 or more.

Feeding
They will take all types of food, but thrive on a wide variety of flakes, frozen and live foods. Live foods such as bloodworm, daphnia, glassworm and tubifex are very good for these fish.

ORIGIN
Man-made

TEMPERATURE RANGE
68–79°F (20–26°C)

COMMUNITY
excellent

ADULT SIZE
female 1 ³/₄ in (4.5cm)
male 1 ³/₄ in (4.5cm)

DIET
all foods

EASE OF KEEPING
10/10

PH RANGE
6.8–7.5

Knife Livebearer / *Alfaro cultratus*

ORIGIN
central america

TEMPERATURE RANGE
73–80.5°F (23–27°C)

COMMUNITY
excellent

ADULT SIZE
female 2 ¹/₂ in (6.5cm)
male 3 in (8cm)

DIET
all foods

EASE OF KEEPING
10/10

PH RANGE
6.8–7.5

This species comes from within the group known as 'Old World Live-bearers'. This variety, among many others, has been known to science for a very long time but because of their plainness compared to other colourful live-bearers, such as guppies and platies, they have largely been forgotten. It is, in fact, a very nice little fish that is very easy to keep and maintain, and it is easy for the novice to learn about the breeding and growing on of the fry. There are specialist societies all over the world specifically keeping this type of fish and they are very easy to find. These societies will give you access to many fish not available to aquarium shops.

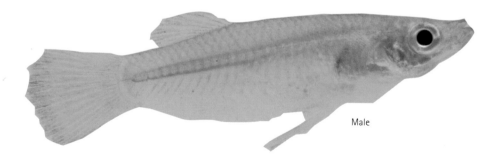

Male

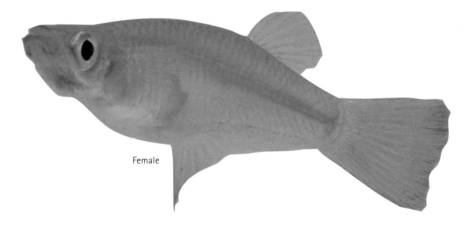

Female

Feeding
They will take all types of food, but thrive on a
wide variety of flakes, frozen and live foods. Live
foods such as bloodworm, daphnia, glassworm
and tubifex are very good for these fish.

Mosquito Fish – Dwarf Top Minnow /
Heterandia formosa

ORIGIN
north america

TEMPERATURE RANGE
70–80.5°F (21–27°F)

COMMUNITY
excellent

ADULT SIZE
female 2 in (5cm)
male 1 in (2.5cm)

DIET
all foods

EASE OF KEEPING
10/10

PH RANGE
6.8–7.5

This fish also comes from within the group known as 'Old World Live-bearers' and again has been known to science for a very long time. Both male and female have black markings in the body and a large black dot in the dorsal fin. They have been introduced into the wild environment in many countries around the world. This is in conjunction with plans for the control of mosquitoes and lowering the level of outbreaks of diseases transferred to humans by mosquitoes. This has never been totally successful but it is how the fish attained one of its common names. They are very hardy and very undemanding.

Feeding
They will take all types of food, but thrive on a wide variety of flakes, frozen and live foods. Live foods such as bloodworm, daphnia, glassworm and tubifex are very good for these fish.

Mudskipper / *Periopthalmus papillio*

To keep this fish you must have areas in the aquarium where the water level is low and the fish can come out of the water and onto solid substrate. In the wild, they come out of river shallows and settle and rest on flat sandy areas looking for food. They can be very aggressive towards each other and it is advisable to only keep one or two in an aquarium together. They are a truly amphibious creature. No differences are known between male and female and breeding by groups has been unsuccessful. When you go to feed them, be careful because they will jump at your hand to take the food.

Feeding

They will take all types of food, but thrive on a wide variety of flakes, frozen and live foods. Live foods such as bloodworm, daphnia, glassworm and tubifex are very good for these fish. Grated beef heart will be readily taken.

ORIGIN
africa

TEMPERATURE RANGE
75–84°F (24–29°C)

COMMUNITY
Non-community

ADULT SIZE
female 10 in (25cm)
male 10 in (25cm)

DIET
all foods

EASE OF KEEPING
9/10

PH RANGE
6.8–7.5

Tyretrack Eel – White Spotted Spiny Eel /
Macrognathus armatus

ORIGIN
asia

TEMPERATURE RANGE
71.5–82°F (22–28°C)

COMMUNITY
community with larger
fish

ADULT SIZE
female 32 in (80cm)
male 32 in (80cm)

DIET
all foods

EASE OF KEEPING
9/10

PH RANGE
6.8–7.5

This fish is normally available in aquarium shops at around 4–6 in (10–15cm) in length. When introduced into your aquarium they will immediately swim to the bottom and, if possible, will go snout first into the substrate and completely bury themselves, with just the very tip of their snout showing. You will find that some of your plants will not stay anchored in the gravel for very long. Given time and patience, you can actually get this fish to accept food direct from your hand. It has no teeth, so cannot bite you. As with all of this type of fish, ensure a tight-fitting cover is on your aquarium.

Feeding
They will take all types of food, but thrive on a wide variety of flakes, frozen and live foods. Live foods such as bloodworm, daphnia, glassworm and tubifex are very good for these fish. Grated beef heart will be readily taken.

Guppies – Millions Fish / *Poecilia reticulata*

Guppies are one of the best known tropical fish in the world and appear in many different colour forms and tail shapes. They are generally very hardy and accept a wide range of conditions in the aquarium. However, because their tail is so delicate, do not add them to a new aquarium during the first six weeks. Sexing is easy because the male has a flowing tail and a highly coloured, well-patterned body, while females are drab by comparison. Males constantly chase the females, so if you wanted to breed selectively, mix the fish with care.

Most commercially bred fish are produced in Far Eastern countries, such as Singapore, Malaysia, Thailand and Sri Lanka. Among the different

ORIGIN
central america

TEMPERATURE RANGE
71.5–79°F (22–26°C)

COMMUNITY
excellent

ADULT SIZE
female 2 ¾ in (7cm)
male 2 in (5cm)

DIET
all foods

EASE OF KEEPING
10/10

PH RANGE
6.8–7.5

Laser Ray

Albino

types of guppy available are roundtail, lyretail, top sword, bottom sword, double sword, pintail, veiltail and many others. Some are only available from specialist breeders but there are a number of specialist guppy or live-bearer societies that are the source of a great deal of information and specialist knowledge.

When pregnant, females have a black blotch at the rear of the belly area, known as a gravid spot. Under normal conditions, the gestation period is between 25 and 35 days. Being a live-bearing fish, as the fry are

Flamingo

Lyretail

Blue Snakeskin

Red Snakeskin

released they are free swimming immediately. They will swim for cover and try to stay hidden for a while. Guppies produce about 70 or 80 young at one time and can bear more than one brood of fry from one fertilisation but numbers of fry will reduce.

Feeding
They will take all types of food, but thrive on a wide variety of flakes, frozen and live foods. Live foods such as bloodworm, daphnia, glassworm and tubifex are very good for these fish.

Endlers Guppy / *Poecilia sp. Endlers*

ORIGIN
central america

TEMPERATURE RANGE
71.5–79°F (22–26°C)

COMMUNITY
excellent

ADULT SIZE
female 2 in (5cm)
male 1 ¹/₂ in (4cm)

DIET
all foods

EASE OF KEEPING
10/10

PH RANGE
6.8–7.5

This fish has been placed in this section because it is believed to be another type of guppy. There is much controversy about them at the moment with some people saying that they are just guppies that have reverted to the wild pattern and colouration, while others are saying that they are a separate species altogether. I just think that they are a very attractive fish and are a worthwhile, colourful addition to your aquarium. The breeding and sexing is exactly the same as for standard guppies.

Feeding

They will take all types of food, but thrive on a wide variety of flakes, frozen and live foods. Live foods such as bloodworm, daphnia, glassworm and tubifex are very good for these fish.

Male

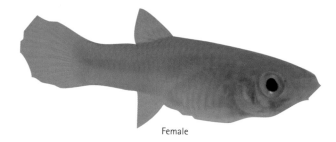

Female

Platy / *Xiphophorus variatus / maculatus*

The platy is another species of tropical fish that is known worldwide. They are very hardy and tolerant to a wide range of conditions in an aquarium, making them ideal to place in a new aquarium. The male has a modified anal fin that is called a gonopodium. Males constantly chase the females, so if you want to breed selectively, mix the fish with care.

Some platies are only available from specialist breeders and may be difficult to acquire. Unfortunately, there is not enough demand to breed them commercially, although a specialist live-bearer society will be a source of valuable information. You can normally find the contacts for these groups in aquatic magazines. Like guppies, pregnant females display a gravid spot on the rear of the belly and gestation is between 28 and 35 days. Between 70 and 80 free-swimming fry are released and swim straight for cover, as there is no parental care for the young fish.

ORIGIN
central america

TEMPERATURE RANGE
71.5–79°F (22–26°C)

COMMUNITY
excellent

ADULT SIZE
female 2 ¾ in (7cm)
male 2 in (5cm)

DIET
all foods

EASE OF KEEPING
10/10

PH RANGE
6.8–7.5

Male – Black Variatus

Female – Black Variatus

Feeding

They will take all types of food, but thrive on a wide variety of flakes, frozen and live foods. Live foods such as bloodworm, daphnia, glassworm and tubifex are very good for these fish.

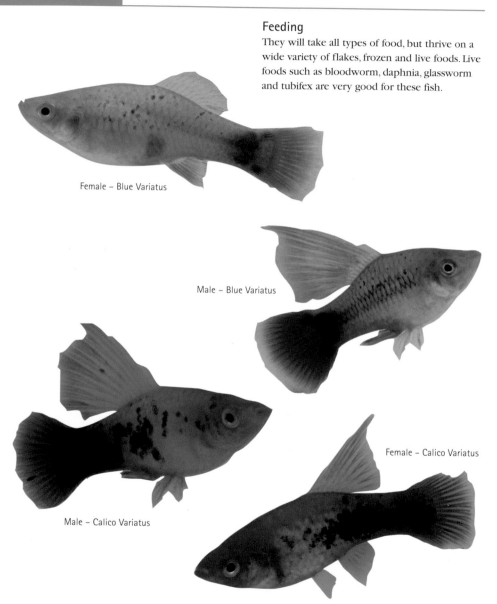

Female – Blue Variatus

Male – Blue Variatus

Female – Calico Variatus

Male – Calico Variatus

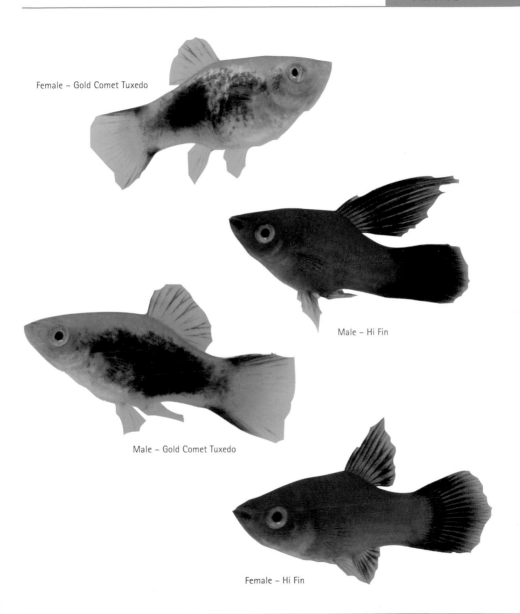

Female – Gold Comet Tuxedo

Male – Hi Fin

Male – Gold Comet Tuxedo

Female – Hi Fin

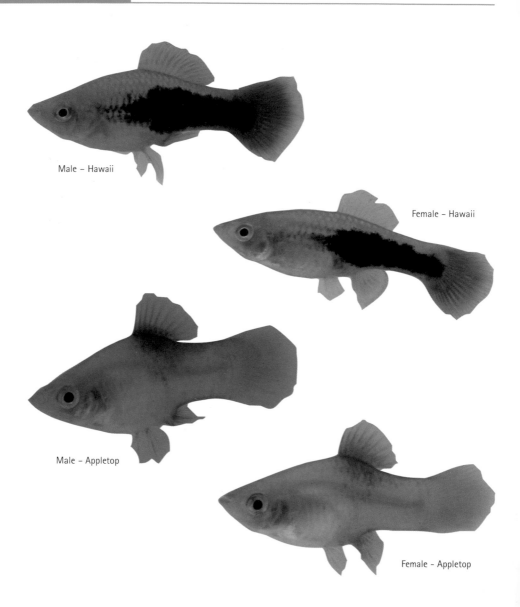

Male – Hawaii

Female – Hawaii

Male – Appletop

Female - Appletop

Swordtail / *Xiphophorus helleri*

The swordtail is another species of tropical fish that is well known worldwide. They are very hardy and tolerant to a wide range of conditions in an aquarium, making them ideal to place in a new aquarium. The male has a modified anal fin that is called a gonopodium. Males constantly chase the females, so if you want to breed selectively, mix the fish with care.

Some swordtail are only available from specialist breeders and may be difficult to acquire. Unfortunately, there is not enough demand to breed them commercially, although a specialist live-bearer society will be a source of valuable information. You can normally find the contacts for these groups in aquatic magazines. Like guppies, pregnant females display a gravid spot on the rear of the belly and gestation is between 28 and 35 days. Between 70 and 80 free-swimming fry are released and swim straight for cover, as there is no parental care for the young fish.

Feeding

They will take all types of food, but thrive on a wide variety of flakes, frozen and live foods. Live foods such as bloodworm, daphnia, glassworm and tubifex are very good for these fish.

ORIGIN
central america

TEMPERATURE RANGE
71.5–79°F (22–26°C)

COMMUNITY
excellent

ADULT SIZE
female 4 ½ in (11cm)
male 4 in (10cm)

DIET
all foods

EASE OF KEEPING
10/10

PH RANGE
6.8–7.5

Male – Gold Spotted

Male – Gold Comet

Female – Gold Comet

Molly / *Poecilia latipinna*

This is another well-known species of tropical fish. They prefer to have a small amount of salt in the aquarium (1 teaspoon per gallon or 4.5 litres). They are prone to 'shimmying', which is caused by shock or chilling of the fish. A salt bath in 1 gallon (4.5 litres) of water from the aquarium, once a day for about 30 minutes for three days should solve this problem. They also suffer occasionally from odinium, which is often mistaken for white spot. A combination of salt and a proprietary medication will easily cure this problem.

Feeding

They will take all types of food, but thrive on a wide variety of flakes, frozen and live foods. Live foods such as bloodworm, daphnia, glassworm and tubifex are very good for these fish.

ORIGIN
central america

TEMPERATURE RANGE
71.5–79°F (22–26°C)

COMMUNITY
excellent

ADULT SIZE
female 4 ¹/₂ in (11cm)
male 4 in (10cm)

DIET
mainly vegetables

EASE OF KEEPING
10/10

PH RANGE
6.8–7.5

Male – Blood Red Molly

Female – Blood Red Molly

OTHER FISH

Black Arowana / *Osteoglossum ferreirai*

ORIGIN
south america

TEMPERATURE RANGE
73–84°F (23–29°C)

COMMUNITY
only with large fish

ADULT SIZE
female 40 in (100cm)
male 40 in (100cm)

DIET
all foods

EASE OF KEEPING
8/10

PH RANGE
6.8–7.5

As this fish grows up to 3 ft (1m) in length, you can see that a very large display aquarium is required. When first imported, this fish is generally only about 3 ¼–4 in (8–10cm) in length but they grow very quickly. They sometimes arrive smaller and may still have an egg sac attached to their body. They are actually feeding from this and it is advisable not to purchase them in this condition. Ensure that the aquarium dealer has them feeding otherwise they can be a major problem. They swim in the upper half of the aquarium just below the surface and will eat anything that lands on the surface. They can and will jump out of the water, so ensure that you always have a tight-fitting cover over your aquarium.

Feeding

They will take all types of food, but thrive on a wide variety of flakes, frozen and live foods. Live foods such as bloodworm, daphnia, glassworm and tubifex are very good for these fish. Lance fish is also an excellent food for them.

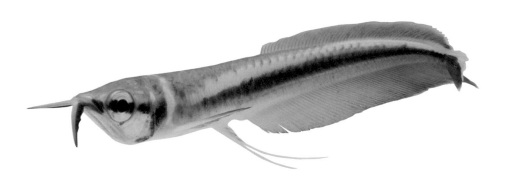

Oscar / *Astronatus occelatus*

Another large fish but they really need to be kept together in a large aquarium. They will eat anything that they can get into their mouth. There are a number of colour varieties of this fish and they can all be kept together without any problem. If you have more than one male in the group there can some squabbling until the dominant male has asserted himself. Generally this is just mouth fighting, where they will lock their mouths together and push each other around in a test of strength until one of them eventually gives up to the other male.

Feeding

They will take all types of food, but thrive on a wide variety of flakes, frozen and live foods. Live foods such as bloodworm, daphnia, glassworm and tubifex are very good for these fish. Lance fish, whole mussels and whole cockles are also excellent foods.

ORIGIN
south america

TEMPERATURE RANGE
71.5–82°F (22–28°C)

COMMUNITY
only with large fish

ADULT SIZE
female 13 $\frac{1}{2}$ in (35cm)
male 13 $\frac{1}{2}$ in (35cm)

DIET
all foods

EASE OF KEEPING
9/10

PH RANGE
6.8–7.5

Common Oscar

Red Oscar

Red Tiger Oscar

Figure 8 Puffer / *Tetraodon palembangensis*

Most puffers have quite diverse markings and this one is no different. It has large, round black spots on the body that are surrounded by what looks like a luminescent yellow-green colouration. The remainder of the body is an off-white-grey colouration. They often swim in a circular motion. When caught and lifted from the aquarium, they inhale air into their stomach and blow up like a balloon until placed back into the aquarium. If a predator attacks them, they can fill their stomach with water and inflate in this way, making themselves look much bigger than they actually are.

Feeding
They will take all types of food, but thrive on a wide variety of flakes, frozen and live foods. Live foods such as bloodworm, daphnia, glassworm and tubifex are very good for these fish. Lance fish, whole mussels and whole cockles are also excellent foods.

ORIGIN
asia

TEMPERATURE RANGE
71.5–82°F (22–28°C)

COMMUNITY
only with larger fish

ADULT SIZE
female 8 in (20cm)
male 8 in (20cm)

DIET
all foods

EASE OF KEEPING
8/10

PH RANGE
6.8–7.5

Red Eyed Puffer / *Tetraodon sp.*

ORIGIN
asia

TEMPERATURE RANGE
71.5–82°F (22–28°C)

COMMUNITY
only with larger fish

ADULT SIZE
female 12 in (30cm)
male 12 in (30cm)

DIET
all foods

EASE OF KEEPING
8/10

PH RANGE
6.8–7.5

This puffer grows rather large and, unless they are well fed, will start to take pieces out of the other inhabitants of the aquarium no matter how large they are. The lips of the mouth are very hard and bone-like so that they can chew just about any type of food offered to them. They will even bite the hand that feeds them, so be careful. The fish has a lovely red ring around the eye and an olive green occellated pattern all over the body. They require a large aquarium to grow to their best. If you keep more than one in an aquarium, you will find that they will constantly nip at each other's fins.

Feeding

They will take all types of food, but thrive on a wide variety of flakes, frozen and live foods. Live foods such as bloodworm, daphnia, glassworm and tubifex are very good for these fish. Lance fish, whole mussels and whole cockles are also excellent foods.

Green Puffer / *Tetraodon nigroviridis*

Puffers are generally very easy to keep and maintain but it is their aggressiveness towards each other and the other fish in your aquarium that are the main problems. If you keep them very well fed on the more solid foods suggested below, the damage to other fish in your aquarium can be reduced to the point of being practically non-existent. Sexual differences on the biggest majority of puffers are unknown and spawning of these fish has been unsuccessful to date. If kept in a species tank, with plenty of bogwood and rockwork, they can be kept successfully. If you have a snail population problem in your aquarium, these fish can be used to great effect.

Feeding

They will take all types of food, but thrive on a wide variety of flakes, frozen and live foods. Live foods such as bloodworm, daphnia, glassworm and tubifex are very good for these fish. Lance fish, whole mussels and whole cockles are also excellent foods.

ORIGIN
asia

TEMPERATURE RANGE
71.5–82°F (22–28°C)

COMMUNITY
only with larger fish

ADULT SIZE
female 7 in (18cm)
male 7 in (18cm)

DIET
all foods

EASE OF KEEPING
8/10

PH RANGE
6.8–7.5

OTHER FISH

Severum – Deacon Cichlid / *Heros severus*

ORIGIN
south america

TEMPERATURE RANGE
71.5–82°F (22–28°C)

COMMUNITY
best with medium to
larger fish

ADULT SIZE
female 8 in (20cm)
male 8 in (20cm)

DIET
all foods

EASE OF KEEPING
8/10

PH RANGE
6.8–7.5

Although they need a large aquarium, these fish will swim around it quite gracefully. When they are young and kept in large groups, there is quite a lot of squabbling but they calm down a lot if reduced to two, or three or a breeding pair. The breeding pair, when ready and conditioned, will clean and spawn on large pieces of slate or rock, or even on the glass walls of the aquarium. They can lay 600-700 eggs in a spawning and they will then take great care of the eggs and the fry when they have hatched out. The breeding pair will set up a territory and if any other fish approach this area, they will chase them away quite voraciously. They will continue to care for the young until they are big enough to fend for themselves or you have lifted them out of the aquarium.

There is the standard form of this fish and also a gold form. They can both be kept together in the same aquarium without any problem; they will even pair up together and form a bonded breeding pair. The resulting fry will be some of the standard and some of the gold form. It is not advisable to keep very small fish in with them but fish such as blue acaras and geophagus, will make ideal tank mates.

Feeding
They will take all types of food, but thrive on a wide variety of flakes, frozen and live foods. Live foods such as bloodworm, daphnia, glassworm and tubifex are very good for these fish. Grated beef heart will be readily accepted.

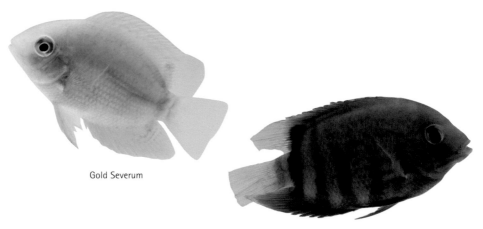

Gold Severum

Green Severum

Marbled Birchir / *Polypterus palmas*

This fish is quite predatory and so must not be kept with small fish. A sandy substrate with plenty of plants, such as straight vallis, onion plants or giant twisted vallis, is ideal for this fish. They can be kept together without any problems. They tend to lie about in amongst the plants waiting for their prey to arrive and will pounce on it in a flash. The colouration of this fish forms an ideal camouflage against a muddy or sandy substrate for this purpose. Fish such as elephant nose, butterfly fish, knife fish and tilapia make ideal tank mates. The male has more rays in the anal fin than the female.

Feeding

They will take all types of food, but thrive on a wide variety of flakes, frozen and live foods. Live foods such as bloodworm, daphnia, glassworm and tubifex are very good for these fish. Grated beef heart will be readily accepted.

ORIGIN
africa

TEMPERATURE RANGE
75–82°F (24–28°C)

COMMUNITY
best with medium to
larger fish

ADULT SIZE
female 12 in (30cm)
male 12 in (30cm)

DIET
all foods

EASE OF KEEPING
8/10

PH RANGE
6.8–7.5

Red Tail Catfish / *Phractocephalus hemilopterus*

ORIGIN
south america

TEMPERATURE RANGE
71.5–80.5°F (22–27°C)

COMMUNITY
species fish only

ADULT SIZE
female 80 in (200cm)
male 80 in (200cm)

DIET
all foods

EASE OF KEEPING
7/10

PH RANGE
6.8–7.5

This is one of the giants. As it grows to 6 ½ ft (2m) in length, you will require an exceptionally large aquarium. The colouration of this fish makes them very attractive to the fish-keeper, especially when seen in the aquarium shop at around 3–3 ½ in (8–9cm). Many people do not realise the potential size of this fish and when it starts to outgrow their aquarium cannot then find another owner because of its size. They are a fish that, even if kept in too small an aquarium, will continue to grow. They will eat anything and everything that is in the aquarium. So my advice is look and appreciate but do not buy, unless you are prepared to keep this fish alone and constantly buy larger aquariums.

Feeding

They will take all types of food, but thrive on a wide variety of flakes, frozen and live foods. Live foods such as bloodworm, daphnia, glassworm and tubifex are very good for these fish. Beef heart will be readily accepted.

Silver Arowana / *Osteoglossum bicirrhosum*

As this fish grows up to over 3 ft (1m) in length, a very large display aquarium is required. When first imported, this fish is generally only about 3-4 in (8-10cm) in length, but they grow very quickly. They sometimes arrive smaller and may still have an egg sac attached to their body. They are actually feeding from this and it is advisable not to purchase them in this condition. Ensure that the aquarium dealer has them feeding otherwise they can be a major problem. They swim in the upper half of the aquarium just below the surface and will eat anything that lands on the surface. They can and will jump out of the water, so ensure that you always have a tight-fitting cover over your aquarium.

Feeding

They will take all types of food, but thrive on a wide variety of flakes, frozen and live foods. Live foods such as bloodworm, daphnia, glassworm and tubifex are very good for these fish. Lance fish is also an excellent food.

ORIGIN
south america

TEMPERATURE RANGE
73–84°F (23–29°C)

COMMUNITY
only with large fish

ADULT SIZE
female 48 in (120cm)
male 48 in (120cm)

DIET
all foods

EASE OF KEEPING
8/10

PH RANGE
6.8–7.5

Tiger Shovelnose Catfish /
Pseudoplatystoma fasciatum

ORIGIN
south america

TEMPERATURE RANGE
73–84°F (23–29°C)

COMMUNITY
only with large fish

ADULT SIZE
female 40 in (100cm)
male 40 in (100cm)

DIET
all foods

EASE OF KEEPING
8/10

PH RANGE
6.8–7.5

As this fish grows up to 3 ft (1m) in length, a very large display aquarium is required. When first imported, this fish is generally only about 3–4 in (8–10cm) in length, but they grow very quickly. The silver and black colouration of this fish makes it very attractive to the fish-keeper. The fish will sit very quietly on the floor of the aquarium with their very long barbels constantly sensing what is happening around it. They are also 'tasting' the water for potential prey. If you keep them well fed on the larger solid foods suggested below, you should have no problems with them.

Feeding
Lance fish, whole mussels, whole cockles, beef heart and large river shrimps will be readily accepted.

Rainbow Snakehead / *Channa sp.*

This fish is very predatory and so must not be kept with small fish. A sandy substrate with plenty of plants, such as straight vallis, onion plants or giant twisted vallis, is ideal for this fish. They tend to lie about in amongst the plants waiting for their prey to arrive and will pounce on it in a flash. This is about the most colourful of this species of fish. Fish such as elephant nose, butterfly fish, knife fish and tilapia can be kept as ideal tank mates.

Feeding
Lance fish, whole mussels, whole cockles, beef heart and large river shrimps will be readily accepted.

ORIGIN
africa

TEMPERATURE RANGE
73–84°F (23–29°C)

COMMUNITY
only with large fish

ADULT SIZE
female 8 in (20cm)
male 8 in (20cm)

DIET
all foods

EASE OF KEEPING
8/10

PH RANGE
6.8–7.5

Blue Lobster / *Procambarus sp.*

ORIGIN
asia (commercially bred)

TEMPERATURE RANGE
73–82°F (23–28°C)

COMMUNITY
only with medium-sized fish

ADULT SIZE
female 4 ³/₄ in (12cm)
male 4 ³/₄in (12cm)

DIET
all foods

EASE OF KEEPING
9/10

PH RANGE
6.8–7.5

Keeping a blue lobster in an aquarium with small fish is not the best thing to do. It will grab anything it can, although it is not very quick. However, it will go looking for the smaller fish when the light is out and the fish are resting. These lobsters are basically scavengers and will eat any food that they find on the bottom of the aquarium. In a good-sized aquarium you can keep a couple of them together but they will set up their own territory and are liable to fight if they meet. Unfortunately, there is very little information about these creatures.

Feeding

They will take all types of food, but thrive on a wide variety of flakes, frozen and live foods. Live foods such as bloodworm, daphnia, glassworm and tubifex are very good for these fish. Lance fish is also an excellent food.

Red Thai Crab / *Sesarma intemedia*

These crabs can be kept very easily but they need to be able to come out of the water. This can be achieved if the aquarium is only half-full of water and a large piece of bogwood is placed in the centre, so that part of it is above the water level. Make sure that the bogwood is not anywhere near the side of the aquarium as the crabs are great escapists. Fish from the size of a platy upwards can easily be kept with them. The crabs prefer a sandy substrate so that they can pick through it looking for morsels of food. They will try to grab hold of any fish if they come too close but they are not normally very successful.

Feeding

They will take all types of food, but thrive on a wide variety of flakes, frozen and live foods. Live foods such as bloodworm, daphnia, glassworm and tubifex are very good for these fish. Lance fish is also an excellent food.

ORIGIN
asia (commercially bred)

TEMPERATURE RANGE
73–82°F (23–28°C)

COMMUNITY
only with medium-sized fish

ADULT SIZE
female 2 in (5cm)
male 2 in (5cm)

DIET
all foods

EASE OF KEEPING
9/10

PH RANGE
6.8–7.5

Rainbow Crab / *Cardisoma armatum*

ORIGIN
africa

TEMPERATURE RANGE
73–82°F (23–28°C)

COMMUNITY
species tank only

ADULT SIZE
female 8 in (20cm)
male 8 in (20cm)

DIET
all foods

EASE OF KEEPING
10/10

PH RANGE
6.8–7.5

These crabs can be kept very easily but again they need to be able to come out of the water. The claws grow quite large and can give you a very painful bite, so be aware when cleaning the aquarium. It is also important to ensure that the lid on your aquarium is a very tight fit, as they will climb anything in the tank and escape. They will also fight each other but normally any damaged claws will re-grow given time. It is very advisable to keep this in a species only tank.

Feeding

They will take all types of food, but thrive on a wide variety of flakes, frozen and live foods. Live foods such as bloodworm and tubifex are very good for these fish. Lance fish is an excellent food. They will also take small pieces of fruit such as apple, grapes etc.

Zebra Apple Snails / *Ampullaria sp.*

There are many different patterns of this snail but unfortunately they are rarely available. They are exceptionally good in a breeding aquarium where the fry are really small because these snails produce infusoria, which is a micro food that can give a good start to young fish. The snails will move up and out of the aquarium onto an overhang and lay their eggs in a cone-like structure, where they will dry out. When the eggs hatch, they just drop straight back into the aquarium and the cycle repeats itself.

Feeding
They will primarily take a small piece of scalded lettuce leaf, boiled peas or spinach.

ORIGIN
asia

TEMPERATURE RANGE
73–82°F (23–28°C)

COMMUNITY
excellent

ADULT SIZE
female 2 in (5cm)
male 2 in (5cm)

DIET
Mainly vegetable foods

EASE OF KEEPING
10/10

PH RANGE
6.8–7.5

BRACKISH

Mono – Fingerfish / *Monodactylus sebae*

ORIGIN
asia/africa

TEMPERATURE RANGE
73–82°F (23–28°C)

COMMUNITY
good

ADULT SIZE
female 10 in (25cm)
male 10 in (25cm)

DIET
all foods

EASE OF KEEPING
8/10

PH RANGE
6.8–7.5

These fish require a brackish to marine water environment in your aquarium. In the wild they seek out freshwater tributaries and streams and then return to the original environment. They can be acclimatised to freshwater in your aquarium but it is not advisable to try and do this permanently. They much prefer to be in a shoal, giving them confidence, moving around the aquarium together. The colouration of this fish is beautiful and a pleasure to watch. They are normally available at around 2–3 in (5–8cm) in length and are slow growers. Differences between male and female are unknown.

Feeding

They will take all types of food, but thrive on a wide variety of flakes, frozen and live foods. Live foods such as bloodworm, daphnia, glassworm and tubifex are very good for these fish. Lance fish is also an excellent food.

Silver Scat – Butterfish / *Selenotoca multifasciatus*

These fish require a brackish to marine water environment in your aquarium. In the wild they seek out freshwater tributaries and streams and then return to their original environment. They can be acclimatised to freshwater in your aquarium but it is not advisable to try and do this permanently. A good filtration system is required for them as they are sensitive to nitrites and ammonia. Because of their potential size and requirements, it is advisable to keep them in a species only tank. Differences between male and female are unknown.

Feeding

They will take all types of food, but thrive on a wide variety of flakes, frozen and live foods. Live foods such as bloodworm, daphnia, glassworm and tubifex are very good for these fish. Lance fish is also an excellent food.

ORIGIN
indonesia

TEMPERATURE RANGE
71.5–82°F (22–28°C)

COMMUNITY
good with larger fish

ADULT SIZE
female 14 in (35.5cm)
male 14 in (35.5cm)

DIET
all foods

EASE OF KEEPING
8/10

PH RANGE
6.8–7.5

Fantails / *Carassius sp.*

ORIGIN
china

TEMPERATURE RANGE
68–77°F (20–25°C)

COMMUNITY
excellent

ADULT SIZE
female 6 in (15cm)
male 6 in (15cm)

DIET
all foods

EASE OF KEEPING
10/10

PH RANGE
6.8–7.5

Most fantails, oranda and goldfish varieties originate in China and some have become more than colour varieties. For example, the pearlscale oranda has raised, pearlised, multi-coloured scales with a very bulbous body. These fish have been selectively bred over many hundreds of years by Chinese breeders. Many people regard the fantails as a pond fish and place them in their pond. This is not advisable. Some will survive the cold winters but many will not. They much prefer warmer temperatures. Good filtration is required to maintain these fish as they produce a large volume of waste matter and so pollution can be a problem. Increased oxygenation is also very important.

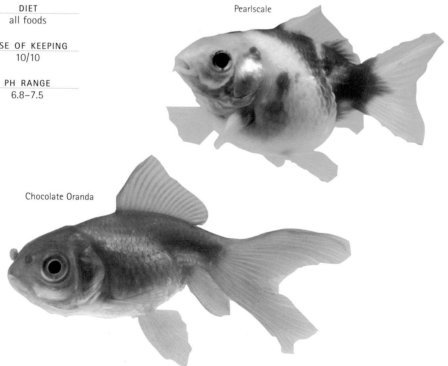

Pearlscale

Chocolate Oranda

Red Cap Oranda

Silver/Blue Oranda

Canary Yellow Goldfish

Goldfish are much happier at the cooler temperatures of your pond and are more liable to survive the winters once they are fully acclimatised. Do not feed the pond fish during the winter period, as this will just heavily pollute the pond.

The shubunkin is a multi-coloured fish with many shades of blue and red. Again this is quite happy to be in the pond at the cooler temperatures.

Feeding

They will take all types of food, but thrive on a wide variety of flakes, frozen and live foods. Live foods such as bloodworm, daphnia, glassworm and tubifex are very good for these fish. Lance fish is also an excellent food.

Shubunkin

Standard Goldfish

Koi Carp / *Cyprinnis carpio*

Japan has been at the forefront of producing the best quality koi carp in the world. They have been selectively breeding these fish for over a thousand years to produce the beautiful colours and patterns that we now see. In recent years, other countries throughout the world have started to breed these fish in commercial quantities but not, as yet, to the same quality as the Japanese. The fish grow quite quickly and you can expect a growth of 4-5 in (10-13cm) per year for the first two or three years. The growth rate will slow down from then on. They require very good quality filtration and high levels of oxygenation to maintain them at their best. Once used to the person who feeds them, they can become very tame.

ORIGIN
japan

TEMPERATURE RANGE
50–68°F (10–20°C)

COMMUNITY
excellent pond fish

ADULT SIZE
female 24 in (60cm)
male 24 in (60cm)

DIET
all foods

EASE OF KEEPING
10/10

PH RANGE
6.8–7.5

Feeding

There are many specialist koi pellets and mixes available and it is advisable to give them a good mix of these foods. Your local koi dealer will advise which is the best available in your area.

Credits and acknowledgements

My heartfelt thanks for their great assistance in the creation of this book must firstly go to my friends and suppliers in Singapore (Pang, Lillian and Karen of Aquarium Iwarna) and my Czechoslovakian supplier and friend (Paul from AquaCzech). They all contributed greatly with the supply of the good quality fish that I asked for. Secondly, many thanks must go to Ross Turner, who, although he works for me as my fish house manager, spent many, many hours of his own time sorting and conditioning the fish and assisting in the photography of them all. Without him, the fish would not have presented themselves as well as they have for the photos in this book.